CONSULTING MADE EASY

All You Need to Know to Get You Started or Back on Track

ADRIAN PARTRIDGE

CONSULTING MADE EASY
ALL YOU NEED TO KNOW TO GET YOU STARTED OR BACK ON TRACK

iUniverse books may be ordered through booksellers or by contacting:

iUniverse
1663 Liberty Drive
Bloomington, IN 47403
www.iuniverse.com
1-800-Authors (1-800-288-4677)

Because of the dynamic nature of the Internet, any web addresses or links contained in this book may have changed since publication and may no longer be valid. The views expressed in this work are solely those of the author and do not necessarily reflect the views of the publisher, and the publisher hereby disclaims any responsibility for them.

Any people depicted in stock imagery provided by Thinkstock are models, and such images are being used for illustrative purposes only. Certain stock imagery © Thinkstock.

ISBN: 978-1-4917-9202-5 (sc)
ISBN: 978-1-4917-9203-2 (hc)
ISBN: 978-1-4917-9201-8 (e)

Library of Congress Control Number: 2016904493

Print information available on the last page.

iUniverse rev. date: 3/31/2016

Dedicated with love to Jennifer, Tom, Ben, and Alex.

And to all you hardworking consultants out
there. I wish you all great success.

CONTENTS

INTRODUCTION

Why Read This Book?

Perhaps you're thinking about setting up your own consulting business. If so, this book tells you what to do and how to do it—and how to be successful from day one. I've put in all the stuff I wish I'd known when I started out.

Or perhaps you're already a consultant and wondering whether there are some gems of information in here that might help you. You'll find plenty of ideas and examples to help you look at your own practice and find ways to do things differently. I hope you can make things better—and make more money.

I've worked as a consultant for more than twenty-five years, in a small consulting company, a large consulting organization and independently. I've also worked in public industry and private industry and seen the work consultants do from the other side.

Over the years, I've seen it all: what to do, what not to do, good clients, bad clients, good consultants, bad consultants, peaks, and troughs. I've had great satisfaction and experienced big problems. I've consulted for tiny companies and multinationals, governments and municipalities. I've worked with presidents and CEOs, factory workers and janitors. All in all, it's been fun, fascinating, continually changing, and always a challenge. I've also been lucky enough to work on three continents and in eighteen countries—all at the clients' expense.

People in many professions try to make their work seem more complicated than it is. Consulting is no exception, and part of that is a protection mechanism. We might think, *When people realize we're not that clever, no one will hire us anymore.* I absolutely don't believe this. There are many, many reasons for using consultants, and wanting someone who is very smart is hardly ever one of them. Consulting is like any other business; learn some simple techniques, and you'll be successful.

That's why I've made this book easy to understand, logical, clear, and succinct. I've addressed the issues that have puzzled or worried me during my consulting career. I've also included lots of examples, advice, and recommendations drawn directly from my experience.

If you've ever thought you could work for yourself, be your own boss, sell your own services, or take control of your destiny, then consulting is an option for you—and this book is for you. If you're already a consultant, there may be a few things in this book that will help you.

So enjoy the book. And welcome to consulting, if you're just starting out. You're entering a valuable service industry filling a critical business need. You're also embarking on an endlessly entertaining and challenging career; I guarantee you won't be bored. So whether you're twenty-five years down the road, like me, or taking your first steps in the business, I wish you success and, above all, a varied, fascinating, and enjoyable career.

CHAPTER 1

What Are Consultants, and What Do They Do?

Let's go right back to basics to start off.

Okay, you're at a party. You've had a couple of drinks, and you're feeling relaxed and sociable. Your host introduces you to a couple you haven't met before, and of course one of their first questions is "And what do you do?"

I'm always tempted to invent something in situations such as these. But you're not me, and although tightrope walker, submarine captain, astronaut, hot-air balloonist, and glamour photographer might enter your mind, you resist. "I'm a consultant," you say in an urbane air (which eludes me at parties).

"A consultant," the man echoes, and they look at each other. There's a pause. Then "And what do you consult in?" So you go on to explain your area of consulting, but you can see they don't really follow. After a while, they make an excuse and go to find the party's resident astronaut.

The vast majority of people don't know what consultants are, what they do, or how they do it. This is strange because most people who work for a large organization come across consultants at some point in their careers.

There are also a number of stock definitions of consultants and consulting, not all of which are complimentary. Here are some:

- specialists who work as temporary employees of companies
- people who borrow your watch to tell you the time
- people who con you and insult you
- people who provide specialist advice for fees
- people who give advice
- people trained to analyze and advise a client in order to help the client

If pushed to define a consultant, I would say it's anyone whose advisory services are purchased by an organization or individual. There's a huge range of subjects you can consult on—from accounting to security, from energy management to IT management, from parties to employee fitness. Maybe this is why people say they don't really understand the term *consultant*: it's too broad.

If a plumber sells a service, is he or she a consultant? Not by most definitions, although you could argue the case. However, the person who does a maintenance survey and recommends hiring a plumber to fix or replace something is definitely a consultant.

So now you're confused and thinking that the guy writing the book can't really define *consultant*. You know what? It doesn't matter. If you can identify a need and persuade others to pay you to help them, that's all that counts.

And How Does the Consulting Business Work?

Consulting is the same as any other service business: you provide a service, and you get paid for it. When I get my hair cut, I make an appointment and go to the salon, and Sarah makes it happen. She always does a good job, and I'm always happy to pay her and happy to return for the same service in a few weeks. Most people wouldn't describe hairdressers as consultants, but the principle is the same.

The many types of consultants work in different ways depending on the type of consulting and the nature of the clients. However, the standard consulting approach is as follows:

- A client is interested in a service you may provide.
- You provide a proposal for the work.
- The client agrees to the proposal and sends you a purchase order.
- You carry out the work and invoice the client (not necessarily in this order).
- The client pays, and everyone's happy.
- Three weeks later, the client calls you again and asks you if you can do some more work.

Of course, there are a whole bunch of issues behind each of the glibly written points above. Simply preparing a proposal covers a multitude of sins by outlining how much you charge, when you'll complete the task, how long it's going to take, and so forth. And do you need a proposal at all?

That's what this book is about. I'll address all of these issues—plus many more.

Why Do Organizations Use Consultants?

Lucky for us consultants or potential consultants, a variety of organizations are interested in us for many reasons. Here are a few, some of which may surprise you:

- You supply a skill that they don't have.
- You supplement staff in a specific area.
- You provide an outside perspective that's perceived to be unavailable within the company.
- You have knowledge of a competitor's approach.
- You're able to work quicker than a staff member.
- Your work is limited, so it isn't worth hiring an employee to do it.
- The organization knows and trusts you and likes working with you.

- You are believed by senior management; sometimes employees aren't.
- Budgets have to be spent by year-end.
- There's a crisis, and they need help quickly.

And hundreds of other reasons. So, particularly in these days of the trend for reduced manpower in organizations, there's no lack of opportunity for consultants. Equally, there's no shortage of available consultants in most fields, so the broader question becomes "Why do organizations use the particular consultants that they work with?"

There are multiple answers to this question. However, in essence, consultant selection is based on

- trust,
- confidence, and
- reputation.

There are a few other related factors that may play into it, such as

- value for money,
- timing, and
- ability to get along with the client.

The key to consulting is putting yourself in clients' shoes. If you can do that successfully, you're in a good position to work out why a client might hire you.

For example, assume you're a manager in a large organization and have a package of work that needs to be carried out by a certain date. It's important that you do a good job and meet a deadline. But you need to contract it out. What do you want?

What you really want is to be able to relax. You want to know that whoever you give it to will produce a high-quality product on time within a budget that you consider reasonable. You want to be kept informed along the way so that if any problems come up, you understand them and know what's being done to get around them. Also, you want to have a professional, enjoyable business relationship with the consultant. And if by hiring the consultant you can end up in a better place—maybe your position in the company is enhanced or the consultant demonstrates a way to get more value out of the business for you than you originally envisaged, then even better.

It's easy, then, for you as a consultant. All you need to do is mentally sit in your client's seat for a while and think what would make things better for him.

Why Would You Want to Be a Consultant?

Well, you're reading this book, or at least flipping through it, so I assume you have at least a passing interest in the subject. But that's a far cry from actually becoming a consultant. I picked up a book on politics the other day, but … perish the thought! Anyway, here are a few things to consider if you're floating the idea of becoming a consultant. It's up to you whether you consider them pluses or minuses.

You get to work with a range of people. Consulting is a people business, so you might get to talk to the CEO one day and the janitor the next.

You get to work with a range of companies. Depending on what you do, you might be speaking with staff at an international manufacturing business one day, a hotel the next, and a municipality the day after. You get to see how they work, what makes them tick, what drives them crazy, and so on. It's fascinating if you like that sort of stuff.

You get to be entrepreneurial. You can use your imagination, put yourself in your clients' shoes, and figure out what will help them. Then you can propose to do that for them.

You get to help people. Consulting should be about more than doing a task for money. You get to enjoy helping people achieve their goals, advance in their positions, and be happier.

You get to charge what you like. This isn't always true if you're working for a consulting company, but that's the deal if you work for yourself. So charge what you think is fair for the value you bring.

You get to invoice for your services and get paid. It's nice to get paid, of course, but it may not be regular payments. And of course there are clients who don't pay on time and need to be chased.

You have to balance your workload. "Falling off a cliff" is a phrase commonly used in consulting circles. It means that you've been working so hard on a project that you haven't had time to think about the next project. So suddenly you've finished project number one and have no work—and no income. Ideally you can devote regular hours each week to developing your business so that doesn't happen. But that's easier said than done.

You can vote with your feet. Most of us sometimes come across people we simply can't stand to be in the same room with. Occasionally that person may be your client. So you get the opportunity to say to yourself at the end of the project, "I will never work with that person again." (Try to last until the end; it's way better for your bank balance.) The couple of times I've done that in my career, it has been really satisfying. If you're a standard employee and that person happens to be your coworker—or worse, your boss—you simply can't do that.

You get to travel at someone else's expense. I've visited eighteen countries in the course of my career, all paid for by someone else. They were places I might never have visited, such as Venezuela, Hungary, and Siberia. It depends what your skill set is, but there are lots of international opportunities if you look in the right places. Of course, Siberia may not be at the top of everyone's bucket list, but to each his (or her) own.

You get to choose when and where you work. Depending on what you do, you may have to visit a client's site from time to time. But aside from that, the client may not care where you are as long as the job gets done. So you can choose to work all night and sleep all day, or blitz the project for one week and then take a week off.

You have to shoulder the responsibility. When things go wrong—your computer dies at the critical moment; you realize after you sent off the report that you made a big mistake; you miss a deadline because you had to rush the cat to the vet; the dog ate your report—it's all down to you. But when things go well, it's all down to you too and what you put in is generally what you get out.

I could go on. Certainly being a consultant is not for everyone. I've worked with people who can't stand the uncertainty of it and people who thrive on that very thing. I've worked with people who get sucked into it and end up working literally all the time, and I've worked with people who limit their consulting to ten hours per week and make a great living out of it. It all depends on who you are, what you want, and what your circumstances are.

How Do I Know If I'm Cut Out to Be a Consultant?

"Well, you'll never know until you try" is a glib, sometimes irritating answer generally accompanied by a patronizing look. You definitely deserve something better than that. Let me ask you a few questions.

- Do you like dealing with a wide range of people?
- Do you cope well with uncertainty?
- Do you thrive on variety?
- Do you like to make your own decisions?
- Are your finances flexible, or do you need a consistent amount of cash each month?
- Do you have a supportive partner?
- Do you like travel?
- Can you adapt to a flexible workload?
- Are you good at shouldering responsibility?
- Can you accept a task that you don't know how to do, confident that you'll figure it out?
- Are you frustrated that the many hours you put in at work seem to make little difference in your pay?

Okay, be honest. Did you answer yes to the majority of those questions? If you did, consulting may be an option for you. It may appeal to you, but that doesn't necessarily mean you should storm into your boss's office tomorrow and tell him to stick something in a certain place (or a variation to that effect). After all, if you do leave and become a consultant, you might want some consulting work from your old employer.

So how do you know if consulting is for you? Reading books about consulting certainly helps, but talking to people can give you a whole new perspective. Maybe you know some consultants who might help if you bribe them with coffee or lunch. (We're easily bribed—or is that just me?) Consultants love giving webinars. Listen to a few in your field of interest. Dig around online, and find out who is consulting on what in your location. In other words, practice as much due diligence as you can.

Also consider the various ways to get into consulting. Depending on your circumstances, maybe you can do part time to start with, as long as you're not in danger of creating a conflict of interest with your current employer. Maybe you don't want to jump into being self-employed but could try working with an established firm of consultants. Or consider going into consulting with a partner or two. Perhaps you're confident of your skills in your field but not interested in marketing and developing your business; in that case, you need an arrangement with someone whose skills lie in those areas.

There are pros and cons to all these options, but the one thing they have in common is that they give you experience in the world of consulting. Also, it's not a one-way trip. I know lots of consultants who've been seduced back to being an employee by an offer from a client. I was one of those people once. I also know consultants who've gone back to their old company in a more senior position after a couple of years of mind-broadening consulting experience.

Am I Smart Enough to Be a Consultant?

Want a simple, straight answer? Yes, you are. Don't ever think otherwise.

If you've ever had a job, someone has paid you for the skills you have, the effort you put in, your ability to work in a team and interact with clients, or whatever the particular aspects of that job were.

Suppose that the company you work for decides it doesn't want a permanent member of its staff in your position anymore. So they "let you go," which is a very irritating way of saying they kick you out. Then, after a few months, they realize (surprise, surprise) that they actually needed someone to do that work. This sort of thing happens all the time, unfortunately.

So if they don't want another member of staff on their payroll, they'll probably contract the work out. And some consulting company will provide someone to fill that role. He will do what you did, with a couple of differences:

- He probably won't be as good as you, not having the background in the organization or the experience that you have.
- He won't be as invested in the job as you were, because it's just another consulting assignment and probably short term.
- He will command a consulting fee that's probably at least double what you were earning. And your ex-company will happily pay that, because they're hiring a consultant.

Who would be the best person to do that job? You, of course! Could you do it as a consultant instead of as an employee? Do I really need to ask?

Think about your current job, a past job, or even someone else's job. When you break a job down, you realize that most of us spend a lot of our time communicating, interacting with people, and doing routine, easy stuff that lots of people could make a good go of. Companies hire consultants for a range of purposes, but the main reasons are that they don't have the time, manpower, or will to do it themselves. Sure, they often need a particular skill set, but they also just need an extra pair of hands. You can be that pair of hands.

I once worked for a gas utility. One of my colleagues was a friendly, gentle guy named Jim. He had worked at the utility for over twenty years and knew everything there was to know about the generation and distribution of gas. When you needed to know something, you asked Jim. He always had time for you, always explained things well, and never ever made you feel that you should have known that already, no matter how true it was.

One day, when the utility was in a downsizing phase, Jim was called in to see the vice president. She told him that his skill set "no longer matches the company's requirements." Just like that, he was let go. I met him for a coffee the following week, and understandably he was very unhappy.

"Have you ever thought of becoming a consultant?" I asked. "You'd be good at it and would probably earn twice what the utility paid you."

He looked at me quizzically. "Me? A consultant? I don't think so." He paused before adding, "I haven't got any consulting skills, and honestly I don't think I'm smart enough."

I thought he was joking. He wasn't. That was really what he believed, this guy who had been consulting within the company for so long. I tried to persuade him, but on that day he would have none of it.

However, my words must have made some sort of an impact, because a few months later I bumped into him in the cafeteria at the utility. Shyly he explained that he'd approached one of his old bosses about some work that he knew needed doing and had been taken on for twenty hours per week on an hourly rate for six months. And, he said, he was enjoying it.

Jim has retired now, but suffice to say that he had his own successful consulting business for seven years and that more than half his work came from the utility that let him go. Not bad for a guy whose skill set was no longer required. And all he needed to do was change his mind-set, which he did successfully.

So, yes, like Jim and thousands of others, you're smart enough.

What Do I Consult On?

There are probably as many answers to this as there are types of consultants out there (not surprisingly), but the answer for a particular individual depends on a couple of things. First, and most obviously, your background and skill set are very relevant here. Second, you must be willing to step outside your comfort zone. Let's take these one at a time by looking at Steve's situation.

For ten years before leaving his current organization, Steve worked in the banking sector. Most recently he was employed by a multinational bank and was engaged in security, helping make sure that the online accounts didn't get hacked into often. Obviously Steve was well suited to do that work for other banks. He knew people in the banking sector, and he knew the terminology, the problems, the solutions, the systems, and so on.

However, if Steve considered other business sectors, he would realize that other companies have online accounts. And when you think about it, that's just about the whole world these days. So if he stepped a little outside his comfort zone, his potential market was huge. And how far he stepped outside his comfort zone was up to him. He could, for example, give training courses to company employees on making their websites more secure or consult software products developers or consult a firm of headhunters looking for employees in the banking sector—or the IT sector.

A consultant I once worked with used to say with irritating frequency, "You go to where the pull is strongest." What he meant is that you make life easy for yourself. You should consult on what you know best, in the sectors that you know well, and in target areas that you know need some assistance. That mantra worked well for him and is actually good advice for anyone, particularly when they're starting out.

When you start, you have no consulting track record, so potential clients can judge you based only on your work experience. It's much easier—much much easier—if they already know you or at least know about you. So who do you know? What could you do that could help them? What were the problems in the company or sector you worked in? What consultants did they use? Maybe you can help the consultants; consulting companies need help too.

Only you really know what will work best for you. And be prepared not to get it right the first time. Do some self-analysis and then get someone who knows you well in a professional capacity to give you some honest opinions. Try the following:

- Write down all your capabilities, be they technical, managerial, administrative, sales, or whatever. And don't forget things like dealing with people, writing well, speaking well, and being positive, organized, and so on.
- List all your qualifications, and include all those boring little training courses your employers sent you on.
- Analyze your track record. Who have you worked for, what have you done, and what are your achievements?
- Who do you know? Dig out all those old business cards, and run back through your e-mails.
- Ask people for honest views on your capabilities. Try to pick those who will tell you what they feel, not what they think you want to hear.
- Now try to pull the main strands of this together into a couple of sentences. For example, "I'm Ian, age thirty-seven, experienced in the retail and light manufacturing sectors with specific expertise in inventory management and logistics. I'm well organized and a good communicator, and I know key people in the transport, plastics, and retail appliance sectors.

All this helps to focus your mind so that you know where the pull is strongest for you. (Okay, I'm never going to use that phrase again.)

One last thing and the most important: *never ever underestimate your abilities.*

It's very easy for most of us to underestimate our abilities, and I speak from personal experience here. When you're struggling and can't seem to get a break, and those little voices in your head are telling you that you're not very good at anything, tell them they're wrong. Actually say it to them (somewhere not too close to anyone). A friend of mine advises thanking them for their input and telling them politely that on this occasion they're incorrect. Whatever you do, try not to hear them, and don't underestimate yourself. Please.

This last point is going to come up a few times in this book: the majority of consultants undersell their services. We'll address that later on.

What Are Some Key Points I Need to Know?

Like any job, being a consultant gets easier the more you do it. I've been consulting for twenty-five years, and I'm still learning. That's part of the fascination. Yet there are a few points I would have liked to learn right at the start.

Cash Is King

I'm sure you've heard this before. It's true for any business and particularly for consulting. Let's face it; you're consulting to earn a living, and you'd like to be paid for the work you put in. Given that, and the fact that you should have a professional relationship with your client, don't be coy about raising the subject when there is a money (or lack of it) problem. Generally the situation is that you've done the work, invoiced, and not received payment. Excuses I've heard to avoid bringing the subject up include "I don't like to talk about money; it sours the relationship" and "Well, it's kind of tacky to bring it up."

I couldn't disagree more. It's a business relationship. If your client takes offense (unlikely), he or she shouldn't be hiring consultants. Try ignoring the plumber or garage mechanic's bill, and see what happens!

Clients Buy Perceived Value

When I started as a consultant in a consulting company many years ago, they assigned me an hourly fee rate. I was supposed to work 80 percent of my billable hours at that rate. I remember being shocked at the time that anyone would ever consider me to be worth so much. (I'm more confident now.) It took me a long time to learn that whatever value I think I'm worth is irrelevant; it's the value that the client perceives he is getting that counts. And when you work as a consultant for a company, the client isn't just hiring you; he's hiring the company with all its reputation, body of expertise, track record, and so on.

The fact that perceived value is critical is never more appropriate than when selling consulting projects. I'll mention much more about that later. First let's explore another key point.

Clients Who Insist on Hourly Rates
Are Generally to Be Avoided

If a client wants a defined piece of work done, it's none of the client's business how many hours I put in. Let's say the client accepts a proposal of $10,000. As long as it's completed to standard and within the timescale, why should the client care if I do it in ten hours or one hundred? Do I care how many hours my decorator took to paint my house? No, I just wanted him to do a good job, and I paid what we agreed.

Quoting hourly rates opens up all sorts of issues, such as the following (all of which I've had thrown at me):

- You'll need more hours than that!
- How can you justify charging so high?
- I was expecting a much lower rate than this.

And the worst:

- I wish I earned that much an hour (conveniently forgetting that they aren't paying for health insurance, sales time, vacation time, etc.).

So avoid quoting hourly rates if you can.

I used to work for a large consulting company that specialized in getting big companies out of environmental disasters. The client's lawyers would call them up and say things like, "We've had a leak and polluted the river. Help!" In cases like these, in which the client wants a get-out-of-jail-free card (literally), you can charge what you want. The consulting company charged very high hourly rates, and the jobs lasted as long as it lasted, sometimes years. Nice work if you can get it.

And one more thing:

Client communication is critical.
Consider two scenarios:

- A client sends you an e-mail with a complicated request. You know it will take at least a week to collect the data and compile it, so you e-mail him back ten days later and wonder why he seems annoyed.

- You've just started a project, and the final report is due in a month. You work hard for more than three weeks, and all is well. You're confident that you'll have the report to your client on time. But he calls you and sounds irritated until you assure him that everything is on track.

Both of these scenarios show a lack of attention to communication. In the first, the client doesn't even know that you received his request, let alone that you're working on it. In the second, he's left to assume that you're working on it, that everything is going okay, and that you'll deliver on time.

In each case, all that's needed is some thoughtful communication. In the first, respond to his e-mail and tell him it will take a few days and that you think you can get him what he needs by a certain date. If he's not happy with that, he'll let you know, and you can discuss it. In the second, all that's needed is a weekly update e-mail or call, something along the lines of "Just a quick update. We have everything we need, and the work is going as planned. We should have the final report with you by the agreed upon date. If you'd like any more information at this stage, please get in touch."

Easy, huh? But those little things make a world of difference, and you wouldn't believe how many consultants don't communicate. Make sure you aren't one of them.

CHAPTER 2

The First Things You Need to Know and Do

Starting out in consulting can be overwhelming. All of it is new; there's so much to do, and it's really hard to know what to start with. The first things you need to know and do ideally come before you even set up your business. They are the basic thought processes, plans, and decisions on which your business will be based. Unfortunately many of us dive in without covering all of this. But that doesn't mean it's too late. It's just better to do it sooner rather than later.

What Do I Want Out of My Consulting Practice?

If I were to levy criticism on those who've taken the big step and become a consultant, I would say that not enough thought went into what they actually wanted out of their consulting practice. Here's a key question—in many ways, it's *the* key question: What do you want?

At one point in my career, I had become so miserable in the large consulting company I was working for that I extricated myself and started my own practice. The main thing I wanted was to get away from the bureaucracy and the constant pressure to meet targets. All the relevant target parameters were posted on an internal spreadsheet available to all, so you could be, and frequently were, criticized for booking only 60 percent of your time to clients that week, criticized for booking only eight hours per day, and so on. Basically the pressure was on all the time. I understand why it was done, and it was a very successful company. It just wasn't a fun place to work.

So think about what you do want. What is your mission statement? What will you look back on and be proud of? How many days per week or weeks per year do you want to work? Who would be your ideal clients? What work do you want to do and enjoy doing? How long do you plan to be a consultant?

It's worth writing all this down and referring to it every now and again. You'll probably make some changes as you get more established. There's nothing wrong with that; it's all part of the process.

What Qualifications Do I Need?

"None and lots" is the short answer to this question. In other words, it depends what we mean by the word *qualifications*.

You don't need a PhD from Harvard or a double first from Oxford. If you have them, great; I'm sure you'll do very well. But consulting is a profession you can enter with no qualifications. There's nothing keeping anyone from calling himself XYZ Consulting and going out and getting consulting work. There are no consulting police that are going to come around and close you down.

Of course it's beneficial to have formal qualifications that you can put on your résumé, so if you have them, don't keep quiet about them. Yet, in my experience, most organizations aren't going to select you based on your qualifications. They're more likely to make that decision based on your track record, whether they know and like you, and whether they feel confident that you'll do a good job for them.

Of course, many consulting assignments require a certain level of qualification—in engineering or accounting, for example. It's worth noting that if you're working in a related or complementary field, lack of qualifications doesn't stop you from working on these projects in partnership with someone who does have the qualifications.

So what qualifications do you need? Well, lots of informal qualifications, which I'd argue are much more important than the formal ones. I've already mentioned a few of these, and here they are again: drive, determination, imagination, listening skills, writing skills, and above all, enthusiasm. If you have all these in spades, there's no way a lack of formal qualifications is going to slow you down.

And finally, if you don't have the qualifications you need in order to get certain consulting assignments, don't stress about it. As a qualified engineer in the United Kingdom, working in a senior position in a large consulting company, I immigrated to Canada to be told that my qualifications didn't count there. Insulted and frustrated, I stressed for far too long about the issue before it occurred to me that, for the majority of work I was doing, I didn't need to be a registered professional engineer. And if that qualification was required, all I needed was to partner with someone who was a PEng. Fifteen years on, I'm still not a PEng, but I subcontract a lot of people who are.

What Fees Should I Charge?

After years of pricing consulting projects, I believe that fee setting is like brewing beer: both an art and a science. You evolve into it with experience. Your fees are per project, per client, and in a competitive situation, based on your knowledge of your competitors. Here are a few points to consider as you price client assignments:

- Fee rates are mainly for you, not the client. As mentioned in the previous chapter, try to avoid telling clients what your fee rate is. They don't need to know unless it's for payment by the hour. For fixed-price projects, where you submit a quote of, say, $25,000, if you do the work in accordance with what's required, why would they care what you charge per hour?

- Where possible, charge based on value if you can calculate it—and generally you can make a good estimate. I'll mention much more about this later. For now, put yourself in your client's shoes. If your client stands to make half a million dollars from your input, paying you $50,000 is a good deal.
- We all have the same number of hours in a day. Just as a starting point, work out the minimum you need per hour if you work twenty hours per week. Then add 50 percent, and make the increased figure the absolute minimum you won't go below.
- Finally, when you start, try to find out what others in your field are charging, just as a guide.

Knowing what to charge as a new consultant is very difficult, even if you have some background in consulting, say, with a big consulting company. Be prepared for a trial-and-error period, during which you overprice some jobs (and lose them) and underprice others. You'll find your level fairly quickly.

Early on in my career, I had two critical lessons on what fees to charge that have influenced my thinking in this area ever since.

I was a relatively junior consultant working for a medium-size consulting company of around one hundred people. The CEO had just sold a consulting project to a well-known organization and was talking to me and a couple of other consultants who were written into the proposal to do the work. He had nearly doubled our usual fee rates, and I made a comment about this. "Adrian," he said, in an arm-around-the-shoulder tone, "they are an international organization and leaders in their sector. It would be an insult to charge them anything less."

In the second instance, I'd just launched my own consulting company and was chatting with Jack, whom I'd always been impressed by. He was twenty-five years my senior and had been my boss many years before. In his late sixties, he still had bright, sparkly blue eyes and a funny story for every occasion.

Jack continued to work a couple of days a week for extremely high fee rates. "I decided long ago," he told me, "that I'd prefer to work one or two days a week at my rates than five days a week at someone else's rates. So that's what I do. I sell value; so if people don't perceive enough value, they don't hire me. Once someone worked out my hourly rate and asked me how I justified charging so much. I told him I didn't need to justify it; you hired me, so you do." Jack has enough people wanting to hire him that he could work five days a week at those rates if he wanted to. He simply chooses to do his work on Mondays and Tuesdays and to enjoy himself the rest of the week. And why not?

Of course, a fee rate is only a part of job pricing. The key factor is the number of hours the job will take. And then there's a whole bunch of other factors to take into account. (See chapter 6 for more fun stuff on this one.)

How Much Money Can I Make?

As a consultant, you can make a lot, or you can make a little. Surprise, surprise.

I know a couple of consultants who have set out to underprice the local market in their field. They get their work mainly by submitting very low quotes for municipality Requests for Proposals (RFPs), and they win quite a few. So they're working a lot and earning very little. On the other hand, I know someone who works one day per week and pulls in over $200,000 per year—nice money if you can get it.

Most of us are somewhere in the middle.

One way to assess how much you may make in the first year is to make a few assumptions and do a few sums. You want a good life from your consulting career, don't you? And you want time for vacations, the family, and not working too many (or any) evenings or weekends. So let's assume the following:

- You work at your basic fee rate for twenty hours per week.
- You work forty-six weeks per year (six weeks of vacation; did you ever have that before?).
- Your basic fee rate is $150 per hour (or pick a number; yours is bound to be different).
- So you earn 20 x $150 per week = $3, 000, and $3,000 x 46 = $138,000 per year.

This is just to give you an idea; the figure of $138,000 may seem low or high to you, depending on who you are, what you do, and so on. It's there just as an example. Hopefully you'll be charging based on what value you provide. And you may well end up getting a higher hourly rate and/or working more hours at that rate.

Really it depends what you want to earn at the end of the day. If you choose to work all the hours God sends, you're likely to earn more. I'd argue that an unbalanced life like that isn't sustainable, but to each to his own.

As you develop your business, your track record, your range of clients, and your consulting expertise, a couple of things happen:

- More work comes to you through referrals, past clients, and so forth. So you don't need to spend so much time getting work in the door.
- You're able to charge higher rates for your work.

So, in theory anyway, things get easier and more lucrative as time goes on. Remember that when the going gets tough.

What Consulting-Speak Do I Need to Know?

If I'm not careful, I'm going to start ranting here. There are two types of consulting-speak:

1. A highly confusing way of peppering your speech with acronyms and meaningless phrases, the main object of which seems to be to baffle the client and everyone else into thinking that you're highly intelligent and know what you're doing, even if you don't.
2. A few terms that are useful but not essential to know and may help when you're dealing with other consultants.

Before I get to the useful stuff (number two), let me give you a couple of examples of what I mean by number one:

> *"The latest analysis is still in IPM, and we may need to peel the onion more before we find out if parameter change is necessary."* (IPM stands for "in production mode," in case you didn't know (and the vast majority of us don't.) The whole sentence really means "We're still working on it, and we may need to do more work than we thought."

And how about this one:

> *"The two analyses have been contemporaneously checked for MECEness."* (MECE stands for "mutually exclusive and completely exhaustive," which of course we all knew.) Overall this means that the two analyses have been thoroughly checked at the same time.

Some consultants seem to be able to talk in confusing jargon and acronyms most of the time. Can I make a plea? Please don't do it. Please. The essence of consulting is communication, and if the way you talk or write is difficult for most people to understand, you aren't doing your job properly.

Okay, now that we've got that out of the way, here are a few terms that might help you:

23

Utilization: This is normally expressed as a percentage and relates to the percentage of the time that you're charging fee rates. For example, if you're 60 percent utilized, that means you're working for a client three days out of every five, on average. It's not a figure that I have a lot of time for, as I'll explain later when project value is discussed; but it's still good to know what it means.

Request for Proposal, or RFP: Many organizations issue an RFP when they want to contract out a project. It's a document describing what they require you to do and what they expect to see in a proposal. (Much more about RFPs later.)

Request for Qualifications, or RFQ: This is much the same as an RFP but issued at an earlier stage. An RFQ is an opportunity to submit a detailed document so that your suitability for making a shortlist can be assessed by the requesting organization. Normally an RFP will be issued to those who make a shortlist.

Fee Rate: The term is fairly self-explanatory, but it may be expressed differently, depending on where you are in the world. When I worked in the United Kingdom, it was typical to quote a daily rate. Elsewhere, an hourly rate is prevalent, like $150 an hour. (Lots more about fee rates later.)

Nondisclosure Agreement, or NDA: Before a company gets into a consulting arrangement with you, they may insist that you sign one of these. Basically it protects them if they feel that you may need access to sensitive data, such as sales figures or general accounts. On signing, you agree not to distribute any of their sensitive information to third parties.

Who Do I Need to Talk To?

Start talking to as many people as you can in your area of expertise—and don't stop when you get better established. The more people you know, the more people you can work with and will want to work with you. You need to talk to lots of people.

We consultants do a lot of talking. Well, most of us anyway. An engineering consultant I know basically seems to dislike people and avoids a conversation if he possibly can. He works for a company that carefully steers him away from most client interactions. And he must be a good engineer, as they've kept him on for years. However, he's the exception. Being antisocial doesn't work for consultants in general, especially not when you're starting out.

So who do you need to talk to? Here are a few ideas:

- ex-colleagues in your area of business
- existing contacts in companies you'd like to work for
- any consultants you know
- people who've started small businesses

You'll probably realize you know lots of people. Run through your old e-mails, business cards, and the like, and make some lists. I suggest prioritizing them A, B, or C, depending on how useful you think they're likely to be. Then target the As first.

If you're feeling short on contacts, the following story may help: As I previously mentioned, I immigrated to Canada from the United Kingdom. I'd been working for a consulting company in the United Kingdom and had a contract to carry on working for them in Canada. However, almost immediately after I left for Canada, they had a change of upper management, and my contract was terminated.

I was left in a new country, with few contacts, and with a family of five to support. Out of necessity, I set up my own consulting company and began the process of simply talking to people. I started by calling a couple of contacts I knew, briefly explaining my situation, and asking them if they could spare twenty minutes to meet for a coffee and give their advice about who I should talk to. I reckoned that *advice* was a good keyword, as most people like to be asked for their advice.

It worked like a dream. Many people spent over an hour with me and gave me up to ten names of people I could contact. Then I called people they recommended, saying, "I was in a meeting with Steve Smith on Tuesday, and he suggested I contact you." Work poured out of this process: I had my first consulting job within three weeks and a six-month contract within six weeks.

I would recommend that process to anyone, particularly if you're just starting out. People are generally happy to help. Remember, the key word is *advice.*

One last point about talking to people: There's a strange rule that seems to apply a lot in consulting. The meetings that you go to with high hopes for a great outcome often turn out to be disappointing. And the meetings you think will be a waste of time often turn out to be the exact opposite. Don't ask me why, but that has happened so often to me that I know it to be true. I guess the moral is that you should keep an open mind.

Do I Need to Talk to People in Elevators?

This is a classic sales technique, and it's your choice. I generally don't, unless I know the person. In fact, I can think of people who I'd really not want to be in an elevator with at all. Of course, what I really mean by this title is "Should I have an elevator speech?" And my advice is yes, you should.

For example, you're at a networking event, and you meet a new person. One of the first things she's likely to ask is "What does your company do?" You should be able to give her a description in a minute or so. With first impressions being so important, how you come over in that minute and what you say are critical. You should be confident; you should be interesting; you should be enthusiastic—and you should be practiced so you don't sound like a bad actor reciting lines.

Most of us have been through the torment that networking events can be. It took me a while to realize that most people dislike them; most people are uncomfortable talking to people they don't know; and some of us run a mile at the thought of them. However, if we've forced ourselves to pluck up the courage to talk to someone, we have in the back of our mind what it's like to be stuck with someone whose elevator speech is bad.

If your body language and tone of voice project boredom and reveal a job or company to be dull, why is anyone going to be interested? If you do that and are employed by an organization, that's bad enough. If it's your own company, it's unforgiveable—worse than not attending the event, in my opinion. As I've said before, consulting is about communication, and if you're communicating negative vibes about your company, you're simply switching potential clients off.

So don't be embarrassed; go for it. Write down three or four key points about your company. Then practice in front of the mirror, talking through them in a way that links them coherently. Try recording yourself and listening to it. Then try it in front of friends and family. Then try it in a business situation, perhaps with a colleague or contact from a previous job. As you get good at it, you're ready for the big bad world of networking events and business in general.

Don't be too hard on yourself. We all have an off day sometimes.

Should I Make My Business Different?

The short answer is yes. You should try to anyway, if for no other reason than you need some way of differentiating yourself from others competing in your space.

If you're starting out in the business, you're at an advantage compared to someone who has worked for established consulting companies and is now setting up on his own. He'll come with a lot of preconceived ideas about what works and what doesn't. While this knowledge can have many advantages in other aspects of running your own consulting show, you're cloning what you know instead of starting afresh.

At the outset of a consulting business—or any business, for that matter— you have the opportunity to shape it how you want it. You can certainly ask yourself what the principles are that you're basing your business on. What are your overall aspirations? What do you want your business to achieve in the broadest terms? Why are you going into business in the first place? What do you want your business to be synonymous with?

What you're doing as you run through these questions is formulating the basic tracks along which you want your business to run. You're coming up with a mission statement and then fleshing it out into something you can base your business on. If you do this and write it down, you have in front of you the key to differentiating your business from the others out there. After all, it's *your* business; you're unique, and your business should be a reflection of you, not of someone you've copied.

You may be thinking that this is easy to suggest in a book like this, but an IT consultant is an IT consultant, a marketing consultant is a marketing consultant, and there are lots of us out there. True, but we're not all the same, are we? We all have our strengths and weaknesses, and we all develop our skills as we go along.

As always, there's lots of stuff online to help you. Some companies specialize in helping businesses differentiate themselves with a view to developing their market share. Here are a few questions to help you, based on some experiences I've had in this area:

- What is your vision for the future of your business?
- What are your business's purposes?
- What are its values?
- What does your business do?
- What are your guidelines (such as honesty, trustworthiness, credibility)?
- What are your commitments (such as delivering fair value or promoting success all around)?
- What is your style (inspirational, fun, communicative)?
- How will you strive to be different?

These can be tough to answer, but they're worth considering at any point in your consulting career.

CHAPTER 3

Setting Up Your Business

Okay, here you are. You've decided to become a consultant. So you need to create your own business. Let's assume you've done at least a little research before you got to this point, and you have some idea of what you'll consult on and some feel for what the demand is for the services you'll offer.

How Do I Set Up My Business?

Setting up a consulting business has much in common with setting up any other type of business. In many ways, it easier, because all you're doing is supplying your expertise. You don't need suppliers, raw materials, industrial space, and so on. You don't even need an office if you're prepared to work from home (which is a good place to start).

So what do you need to be able to accept and carry out consulting work? At its most basic, you need

- a registered company name and address,
- tax numbers (this differs hugely, depending on where you are),
- an e-mail address,
- a company bank account, and
- insurance.

Without these prerequisites, it's difficult for anyone to give you a consulting project. And you want potential customers to have as few barriers as possible.

Honestly it's easy to set up a business, even if you don't have a clue how to do it (and I didn't when I started). Just google "setting up a business in (insert location)," and you'll find a lot of resources to help you. For example, in my area, Small Business BC is dedicated to helping small businesses with every aspect of setup and development. You can likely find the same sort of resources where you live. Go and visit with one of those groups, talk to a few people, follow the step-by-step instructions, pay out some cash, and congratulate yourself. You're now a small-business owner.

Okay, so now the business exists as an entity, and now you can start working. "Yes, but …" I hear you say. "How about a website, logo, business cards, and so on?" Yes, you need all these, but they aren't the priority that many people think they are.

It would be really nice to have some fees rolling in from day one, wouldn't it? So what's the easiest way to earn some fees? Maybe you can get some work from your old company, somebody you already know, perhaps an colleague. If they already know you and understand that you're just starting, they won't be concerned that you don't have all your ducks in a row yet.

It's strange to me that many think the first thing to do in their business is to set up a website. Certainly you'll need a website fairly early on, but the first thing? I don't think so. A website functions primarily as a marketing tool (*not* a sales tool usually; more about that later). I'm not denying the benefits of a website, but it costs money, is time consuming to set up and maintain, and doesn't in itself bring work in the door (usually). My advice is to concentrate on taking actions to start earning some fees initially, and set up a website a little further down the line.

Do I Need a Business Plan?

Yes, you do need a business plan to the extent that

- you've thought about your business and have some ideas of what you hope to earn;
- you've researched and know and understand the niche you're working in;
- you know where your ideal clients are and who they are, and you have some ideas on how to interact with them;
- you've set down some parameters for yourself regarding hours of work, vacation time, and so on; and
- you know how you're going to run your business.

One good thing about setting up as a consultant is that you don't (in most cases) need a highly detailed plan to take to a bank or potential investors, because the costs involved in setting up are usually minimal.

So, yes, you need a plan. Do you need to spend a lot of time on it? I would say no.

A business plan is just that: a plan. As we all know, you can plan all you want, but that doesn't mean things will follow your plan. Particularly when you're starting out in consulting, things will be harder to predict than when you're a few months or years down the line. So the plan you spent so much time formulating in your first week or two may bear little resemblance to what happens later on.

I worked with a consultant who was almost fanatical about planning. (Hard to imagine, I know.) He spent a lot of time planning—to the extent that I wondered how he ever did any actual work. Once he'd produced a detailed plan (they were all very detailed), he stuck to it slavishly. He did okay, but I always thought it was a mistake that he regarded his plan as something that had to be followed to the letter. After all, things change all the time, and in the consulting world, opportunities arise that you can't predict when you're sweating over spreadsheet number seventeen. I guess we're just different; it worked for him, sort of.

As I look back on when I started out as an independent consultant, I see that I wasted a lot of time downloading sample business plans and trying to prepare a detailed one for my business. I would have used that time better by interacting with potential clients. Copying my consultant friend was definitely not for me, nor is it for most consultants.

How Much Money Will I Need to Start With?

As mentioned above, one of the great things about setting up as a consultant is that you don't need a lot of cash to get started. A friend of mine just set up his own consulting business for a grand total of $150. He's working from home, and he already owned a laptop and phone and had Internet access. His area of work doesn't need specialist equipment, so setting up cost him very little. It was the same for me when I started out. That being said, there are a couple of things to consider you may need money for as you start out.

You may want to incorporate your company from the start. This makes it easier to get work from major corporations. If you decide to go down that route, it will cost you. You may want to involve a lawyer and therefore will incur legal fees on top of that.

Hopefully you'll start getting work fairly quickly, but it may be a while before you get paid. A consultant friend of mine has a major contract with a large organization that's very lucrative for him. The only downside is that they consistently take between two and three months to pay each of his invoices. He puts up with it because of the rates he's earning, but if that was his first contract, he would be needing a float to cover his expenses for at least three months. Plan on doing the same when you start out. Hopefully you won't need it all, but just in case …

Should I Do Everything Myself?

Have you ever heard the phrase "working on the business instead of in it"? It refers to a common problem in small business: the business owner trying to do everything, usually to save money. So she works night and day, spending a lot of time doing activities that could be done much more cost-effectively by someone else.

There are things that we simply have to pay other people to do. Have you ever tried your own dentistry? No, I haven't either. Well, apart from … no. And then there are things that you could do yourself. For example, if you're mechanically inclined, you may be able to repair your own car. But is it worth the time, effort, and hassle to do it? For most of us, the answer is no.

Now consider a business example. Would you do your own business accounting? Unless you're skilled in that area, I would say no. It's going to take you a lot of time to figure it out. Then you're not sure whether the assumptions you've made are correct. Then you have to submit tax returns and possibly be audited based on what you've done. There are people who specialize in this stuff; pay one of them to do it.

You've gone into consulting because you have a skill set that's marketable, and people are prepared to pay you for. If you can earn $150 an hour doing what you're good at, why waste your time doing something you can pay someone else a much lower rate to cover. Also, do you even *want* to do this other stuff? Would you enjoy doing the books, trying to set up your own website, fixing your own car, repairing your own laptop? If you love one of these activities, go ahead. But bear in mind that it may not be a cost-effective use of your time.

Why have you become a consultant in the first place? I bet one of the points on your initial plan wasn't to end up spending many hours doing activities that you're not good at and don't enjoy. So please don't try to do everything yourself; in my experience, it's bad for business and worse for your blood pressure.

How about Insurance and Liability?

An electrical engineering consultant once got the sort of call we all dread. It started with the words "I hope you're well insured." A monitoring instrument he had set up on a client's site had caused an electrical short and set up a chain of problems that ended with lights failing on a major highway and a traffic accident (no one was hurt, thankfully). Or that was the story anyway. In the end, it had nothing to do with the instrument, but he didn't know that at the time. And although he was well insured, he had a few sleepless nights until it was sorted out.

I guess we can all come up with some sort of weird chain of events that resulted in a disaster. My point is that stuff happens, so stinting on insurance is not a good idea. You need to be covered, and you need to be covered well, particularly as we are living in an ever more litigious world.

So find out what coverage is typical in your profession. What you're consulting on will determine how much coverage you need. It's worth doing some shopping around before you commit to a particular company. Running your consulting business will give you enough concerns without worrying about your insurance coverage. So once you've got it in place, take a deep breath and move on with everything else.

How Long Will It Take to Get Up and Running?

The good news is … not long at all. In fact, it will take as long as you let it. For example, if you decide you have to have the best website ever before you get going, it'll be quite a long time. But if you're more practical (and dare I say professional?), you can be earning fees very early on while spending a little time here and there sorting all the bits and pieces out with the basics of your business.

By the time a month has elapsed, I would expect you to have most of it in place. There will be things that you'll want to improve and develop, such as your website and marketing material. These tend to need attention from time to time for as long as you're in business. But the basics, such as your company setup, bank account, bookkeeping, and insurance, should be in place and not need a lot of input from you.

So you now have your own business, a going concern. All you need to do then is run it. And that's what the rest of this book is about.

CHAPTER 4

Looking Out for Number One

Strangely you won't find anything about looking out for number one in many books. I think that's strange because if you don't have some strategies and techniques for keeping yourself fit, motivated, and able to do all the things you need to do, everything else is a waste of time.

When we count our blessings, most people count their health as number one. And that means physical and mental health. Try writing a report when you're feeling miserable, for example. It's really tough. So please don't skip this chapter. It's critical!

Isn't Health the Most Important Thing?

You've read this far in the book, so I'm going to stick my neck out and suggest that you've dared to dream. Maybe you're already consulting, or you're in process of setting up, with day one just around the corner. Or maybe it's all in your mind but there's that little thrill going through you as you think ahead of all the good things that are going to come out of your enterprise.

I don't want to pour cold water on any of this. I wrote this book to encourage people into the profession with the hope that they'll get all the great experiences I've had and more. But we have to be realistic, and we have to be practical. It's very easy to get so swept up in things that you can't take a vacation anymore. Or you lose that time you set aside for the gym and can hardly even stop for lunch. How did that happen? That wasn't part of the plan.

So, to answer the subtitle question, yes, health is the most important thing, because without it you can't be a consultant—or anything else for that matter. If you're self-employed or running a small company, no one does your work when you're ill, and no one pays you. So maintaining your health is critical. Yet it's surprising how little attention most people pay to it.

So here's advice: give matters related to your health the same weight as anything else—be it doctors appointments, gym time, you time, lunch breaks, or time off. It's easy in a flexible, variable business like consulting to prioritize work over everything else. That's how you start to miss the gym, your breaks, and so on—and in the end lose your health. And who wants that?

We've been discussing personal health, but how about relational health? Once you start prioritizing work over everything, your daughter's soccer matches, your son's piano recitals, or nights out with your partner take a lower priority. And surprise, surprise: that all flows back to having an adverse effect on your personal health.

If you're reading this thinking, *Yeah, yeah, tell me something I don't know*, be warned how easy it is to fall into this trap when you're consulting. I know, it has happened to me, despite all my best intentions. It creeps up on you over a period of months or years. I've also seen it happen to many people I've worked with, most of whom have either denied it or laughed it off when I've confronted them. So make sure you don't become one of them.

Who Is Supporting Me?

Starting a consulting business or keeping an existing business going isn't the easiest thing to do. We've already talked about all the benefits, but being a consultant is essentially living on your wits, and that can be difficult, particularly when you start. I'd argue that it's harder than that job at the multinational or at the local municipality that you used to have. (Remember why you left?) On the other hand, it's fascinating being a consultant, but that doesn't mean it's a bed of roses.

Okay, it can be tough at times, but it's doubly tough if you don't have support. If your partner isn't happy with what you're doing or your personal situation doesn't lend itself to the hours you're trying to keep, this makes things very difficult. In a way, it's harder than when your work clashed with family issues when you worked for that company. Then you had an organization demanding certain things of you, and you had to comply (to an extent anyway). Now you're making all the decisions, which can be tough to explain to someone who isn't involved in or familiar with your business.

So it's worth at least thinking about what support you have and discussing everything with your significant other. And let's get things in the right order here. At the end of the day, your significant other is more important than your consulting business. Try to work out some ground rules regarding your business that work well with your personal life—and stick to them.

How Do I Keep Positive and Motivated?

Someone once described consulting to me as "throwing balls up in the air one at a time and waiting for them to come down." No, he hadn't lost the plot entirely (although he went on to do exactly that later in his career, but that's another story). What he meant was that you keep on contacting potential clients, submitting proposals, and chasing leads until you get some work. On balance, that's a valid description of the sales process of consulting.

What Ted (for that was his name, and still is I believe) didn't include in his description was how to deal with the situation when all the balls are floating out of reach, and it seems like none of them will ever drop back down to you. At that point, it's very easy to become negative and demotivated, especially if you're working alone. As we all know, when you're feeling miserable, it's very hard to do anything and extremely easy to put things off until you feel better, whenever that is. In the meantime, you look at your cash flow and forward workload and get even more depressed.

If you've ever been mired in problems, you're all too familiar with what those little voices in your ear are whispering. Actually they're not whispering; they're shouting. "It's all going wrong! Get out before it's too late! You didn't really think you could make this work in the long-run, did you? Why are you putting yourself through this? You could just get a job; in fact, you should never have left your job in the first place." And so on and so on. And it's Monday morning, and you wonder if you look as depressed as you feel. If only you could get your mojo back, maybe you could get out of this mess.

Winston Churchill once said that success is "walking from failure to failure with no loss of enthusiasm." Obviously, staying motivated wasn't a problem for him, although apparently even he suffered from what he termed "the black dog of depression" from time to time. But how do we mere mortals keep motivated when things are going wrong and the voices are yelling negative thoughts in our ears. I guess that depends on who you are, because we all deal with this stuff differently. Perhaps one way to start coping a little better is understanding where those voices are coming from.

Our brains' overriding function is to keep us safe, and that includes a multitude of amazing capabilities, such as the ability to close our eyes before something hits them, even when we don't even register seeing anything. The brain reacts to any form of perceived danger, including stress because you're worried about your business. So your brain tries to get you back to a state of safety. Perhaps you stepped away from that safe place when you launched your business, and while things were ticking along, it was okay. Now things are much harder, and your brain wants you back in that safe place. Hence the voices.

Now, this may sound a little hokey, but you could argue that just ignoring these voices is being disrespectful to yourself. After all, they're part of your built-in wiring, and they're coming from a good place: they're trying to keep you safe. Crazy as it may sound, having a reasoned conversation with them may help. Instead of letting them get you down, in which case they tend to get louder, debate the issues with yourself. You may feel better.

For example, if your inner voice is telling you to pack it all in and go back to your old job, you may gently remind yourself that you were very unhappy in your old job, because you were bored and unfulfilled. Also, recall how exciting it was when you started your business and how great you felt when things were going well. After all, it was a reasoned, thought-out choice you made when you decided to start your business.

You know what you need to do to get things back on track, and it's all stuff that you've done successfully before. So throwing everything away and finding a job isn't going to make you happy; it's going to make you more stressed. So you can thank your inner voice for its input, but inform it that you've decided not to take that option.

Aside from telling your inner voice that you know better, what else can you do? Here are a few things that have helped me over the years.

- Do your very best not to fall off a cliff. As described earlier, falling off a cliff is what happens when you work full time on a project or projects for a period of time, and when they end, you suddenly haven't got anything to do. The solution to this is to make sure that however busy you are, you devote at least 20 percent of your time to bringing in more business.
- Try to find a mentor, business coach, or confidant. This can be anyone you like, who has a good understanding of consulting, and who you can talk openly and honestly with about your business. Finding that person can be critical for a whole variety of reasons, not just helping you when things aren't working out.
- It's easier said than done, but concentrate on not stressing about your lack of work or whatever is depressing you. Here's a

phenomenon that's hard to explain: at the times you most want to get work, you're least likely to get it. When you're so busy that you'd be relieved if you didn't get that extra work, you're guaranteed to get it. Don't ask me why; that's just the way it is. So if you can force your mind into a "I don't really care if I get this project or not" attitude, your chances of getting it are much better.

- Go and exercise—hard. Do whatever works for you: walk, run, swim, bungee jump, pothole, climb frozen waterfalls. Whatever it is, come back exhausted, and I promise you'll feel a little better. I get all my best ideas when I'm running. For you, inspiration and positivity may come in the middle of a bungee fall or halfway up the ice cliff. Just get out there and give it a go.

- Review the work you've done. You got that work; you can get more. How did you get that work? Did you ask for referrals? It's not too late; try it now.

- Cultivate a group of consultants. Go for coffee with them individually to talk about business in general. Ask them what they do in your situation. At worst, just have someone to chat with over coffee. That's better than gazing miserably at your laptop or phone and not doing anything.

- Take a day off. Go on, give yourself permission, and take the whole day off. And try not to think about work. When you catch your mind going back to your problems, tell yourself not to do it.

- And above all, remember that this negativity, this set of problems is temporary. It will pass. It will!

Am I Going to Get Lonely?

I have certainly been lonely at times during my consulting career, and chances are you will too. This is particularly the case if you're a sole operator, a company of one. Of course, it depends on how you deal with a lack of human interaction.

If your work takes you out to other companies, clients' sites, or meetings, loneliness probably won't be a problem for you. But if most of your work is online or home-office based, you may have a problem. Don't underrate that problem, because it can lead to demotivation. And if you read the previous section, you have some ideas for overcoming that. But prevention is better than cure, so the issue of loneliness is worth thinking about and dealing with before you start climbing the walls.

It's obviously cheaper to work at home, but many consultants prefer to rent a desk in a larger office so they get human contact. You may not know Jennifer, Steve, or Andrea very well, but it's good to chat with them for a minute at the watercooler or in the kitchen while you make coffee. It's also good to be able to hear other people moving around, talking, making calls, and so on, as you work on your own stuff—if you're someone who misses that sort of thing. While working in multifunction workspaces, I've also found it very interesting to hear what businesses other people run. You may even get a useful lead.

Another option (and yes, I've done this too) is to grab your laptop and work in your local coffee shop. It's noisy and difficult to concentrate there, and you'll probably get less work done, but something about the flow of people and their proximity has helped me when I'm feeling lonely. As I think about it, I've probably gotten more work done as a result, because I've felt better when I got back to the home office.

We're all different, and only you know how much of a problem loneliness will be for you. Most consultants I know cope with it well yet admit that it's a factor on occasions. And like other issues, it can sneak on you over time. Maybe working at home has been fine for six months, but now you can't bear the thought of going into your office on Monday morning. If that's the case, address the problem, and do something about it. It may mean simply rescheduling so you're out at a meeting most days. Or just try the Starbucks office. Or both. You'll sort it out; most of us do.

How Do I Cope When Things Are Going Badly?

All of us have to deal with this question, and not just in relation to our business. I've covered this to an extent a few sections earlier in the discussion on how to stay positive and motivated. However, this is different. There can be nothing wrong with your motivation, yet things can still be going badly in your business. So how do you deal with it? What do you do? And how do you make sure it doesn't get you down in the long-run?

A business, like anything, goes through good and bad patches. In a consulting business, you're primarily dealing with people, and they have their ups and downs, issues, foibles, and so on. Catch a client at the wrong time, and for no fault of your own, you may end up with a problem in your business. How you deal with this stuff is critical.

As I look back over my consulting career, at any point in time I've had various clients I'm working with. Most of the time there's an issue with at least one of them. It may be as simple as them wanting a little more information in a particular part of a report I sent, or they have a problem with my invoice for some reason, or they haven't paid when they said they would. Most of these problems are easy to resolve, and the key is to deal with them in a reasonable way before they become significant issues. In themselves, they don't constitute "things going badly," but them can mount up if you let them.

It's worth analyzing what we mean when we say that things are going badly. Is it lack of work? Is it cash-flow problems? Is it staff or subcontractor issues? Is it a couple of clients giving you a hard time? Is it simply you overreacting to something that has happened? As most of us have a tendency to focus on the negative, take time to consider what's going well in your business. In my experience, more things are going well than are going badly. So make a list of what's going well and another list of what's going badly. At least then, as you review the lists, you'll get a balanced view.

Let's say you've done this, and you identified two or three things that are causing things to "go badly." Now put them in order. Which one is causing you the most grief, costing you the most money, keeping you awake at night?

Once you can address them one at a time, starting with the most problematic, start asking yourself a number of questions. I suggest writing down the questions and your answers so you can refer to them now and in the future. What can you do to make things better? Who could help you? Who could you talk to? Why is it happening? Has it been a recurring problem? What fixed it last time it happened? What can you do to prevent it happening again? What happens if you do nothing? Does it get worse or stay the same—or even go away?

The outcome of this analysis is likely to be a list of actions. Once you have this list, run through it, and make sure each action is specific. For example, "I need to sell more work" is a general objective, not a specific one. "Contact Steve Jones at XYZ Company and suggest an extension to the previous project we did for him" is the type of specific action that should be on your list. For each of these specific actions, assign a timescale. For example, "Contact Steve Jones by April 15." Then all you need to do is stick to your self-imposed list of actions.

This sort of analysis has worked well for me. It's an analytical approach as opposed to an emotional response to the feeling that "things are going badly." Once you've worked it through, you're actively doing something to make it better, which should make you feel better too.

How Should I Manage My Time?

It has always been puzzling to me how free many businesspeople are with their time and what a low value they give it. Time is the one thing we all have the same amount of each day, yet many businesspeople seem to lose track of the importance of it.

As stated before, it's very easy to let your business get out of control and take you over—that is, take up all your time. I believe you have to be firm about the time you're prepared to commit to your business. If, at the outset, you decide you want to work no more than forty hours per week and have six weeks vacation per year, that's your decision. You should stick to it all the time, apart from in exceptional circumstances. And even then you have to make sure that "exceptional circumstances" doesn't gradually change into "everyday circumstances."

It's often easier to track your time in consulting than in many other professions. In many cases, you may be building up the costs for a potential project based on how long you think it will take you (as well as a host of other factors). So if you decide that you'll spend 100 hours on the project at $200 an hour, you may propose a fixed cost of $20,000 for the work. If you track your hours spent when you do the work and find it took 150 hours, you're effectively working for $133 an hour. You're not earning any more overall; you're just eating up time that you could have used for other work. But if you broke your rules, you may have eaten into family time, your weekend, your vacation, or whatever—none of which was part of you plan.

So tracking your time spent is a critical part of consulting, even if you're only tracking your own time. And anyone who has worked for a consulting company can tell you how they emphasize time management so they can maintain company profit margins. They don't mind you working on weekends.

Time management is a major way to help you keep your sanity. It also provides you with a lot of useful information about your business. If you track your time and realize you haven't put any significant effort into sales or marketing recently, you may have been steaming toward the cliff edge without any brakes. And we all know what that means.

Only you know how to break up your week to best effect for your business. And that will vary according to how long you've been in business, how successful you are, and a number of other factors. A typical breakdown might look like this:

- work for fees: 50 percent
- sales prospects, proposals, prospective client meetings: 20 percent

- marketing, networking: 20 percent
- administration, training, other: 10 percent

If you're starting out and don't have much work coming in, you may be spending 60 to 80 percent of your time on sales, marketing, and networking. On the other hand, if your business is mature and referrals float in the door regularly, perhaps a couple of hours per week can keep things ticking on the sales and marketing front. Just make sure one sector of the pie doesn't take over.

One final point: A consulting friend of mine once complained to me that he worked twelve-hour days and weekends, and there were still things he hadn't done. He confessed that as he drove home from his office, he felt depressed because he still hadn't covered everything he needed to. "Gerry," I replied, "with respect, I think you've got this around the wrong way. You'll never finish everything that needs to be done. Never. It's an unrealistic goal. Instead of getting depressed about what you haven't done, why not use your journey home to celebrate what you have done?"

This seemed to strike a chord with him at the time, and I'm glad to report that he changed his attitude and was happier. I'm not so glad to report, however, that when I met him a couple of months later, he was back to moaning about not completing stuff. I thought it was good advice; I guess he just chose not to hang onto it.

How Do I Keep It All in Perspective?

All of us get things out of proportion and lose perspective. We've already discussed keeping the whole business in perspective and that, at the end of the day, it is *not* more important than your significant other, your children, or your health. But how about the actual business itself? Losing perspective on certain parts of the business can have an effect outside your work. Here are some techniques that have helped me over the years:

- You really don't like working with this client. They're difficult, demanding, and unpleasant. In an effort to keep them happy (probably unsuccessful), you're devoting a disproportionate amount of time to them.

Well, stop! Analyze what this relationship is worth to you. Can you survive without it? How important is it relative to clients you like working with? In every situation where I've done this analysis, I've reached the conclusion that I can manage without more work from the client. Once you've decided that, it's like a weight off your mind. All you need to do is put up with them until the project is over. Then you can never interact with them again. It's a great feeling.

- You've bitten off more than you can chew. The project is going horribly wrong; you don't know if you'll be able to complete it; you find yourself stressing badly and as a result falling even further behind.

Take a deep breath, and step back for a moment. Consider what would happen if you goofed up completely and the client either fired you or would never work with you again. Is that the end of your life? No. Is it the end of your business? No. Will it be uncomfortable, embarrassing, damaging to your reputation? Yes, probably, but all these are temporary things. It's certainly not the end of the world. The sun will rise tomorrow.

I've found that thinking along these lines helps me gain perspective, calm down, and get in a better position to rectify problems. And please go and talk to your client about the issues. People are generally more sympathetic and understanding than we think they will be.

- Your tenth proposal in a row has failed to sell. Now work is running out or has already run out. Whatever you do, you can't seem to turn things around. You're depressed and getting desperate.

Okay, let's get this in perspective. First, just about every consultant has been in this position at some time or another, so you aren't alone. Second, there's little logic to sales success. It's like betting on black at roulette because the last ten spins all ended up red. There's no more reason that the next one should be black than the ten previous ones. Correspondingly, there's no reason your eleventh proposal shouldn't sell just because the others didn't.

Remember, you got work in the door previously, and you will again. So my advice is to try not to let a run of bad luck affect you too much. (Easy to say, I know). Stuff happens; it's not a fundamental shift. Work will come in again, and for some perverse reason, it's more likely to come the more relaxed you are about it.

My father had a saying that never failed to irritate my mother. Actually he had a few, but this one is relevant here. He would generally use it when she was stressing over something that he considered to be of minor importance. With a slight shrug of his shoulders and a faint smile, he'd say, "It will all be the same in a thousand years, Margaret." Take from that what you will. I've often tried to think of it when I'm getting wound up. By the way, my parents were married for more than forty years, so I guess he didn't irritate her too much.

CHAPTER 5

Marketing

Yes, we all know what the word *marketing* means, don't we? Or do we? How does it differ from *sales*? Is a website a marketing tool? Is networking part of marketing? How about training courses you might go on?

Marketing means different things to different people, so let's start by defining what we mean. If you look up marketing in businessdictionary. com, you get the following:

> The management process through which goods and services move from concept to the customer. It includes the coordination of four elements called the 4 Ps of marketing:
>
> 1. identification, selection and development of a *product*.
> 2. determination of its *price*.
> 3. selection of a distribution channel to reach the customer's *place*.
> 4. development and implementation of a *promotional strategy*. ...
>
> Marketing is based on thinking about the business in terms of customer needs and their satisfaction. Marketing

differs from selling because (in the words of Harvard Business School's retired professor of marketing Theodore C. Levitt)

Selling concerns itself with the tricks and techniques of getting people to exchange their cash for your product. It is not concerned with the values that the exchange is all about. And it does not, as marketing invariably does, view the entire business process as consisting of a tightly integrated effort to discover, create, arouse and satisfy customer needs.

In other words, marketing has less to do with getting customers to pay for your product than it does with developing a demand for that product and fulfilling the customer's needs.

Still confused? Hopefully the next sections will clarify things a bit more for you. From a consultant's perspective, try thinking of marketing as anything that develops demand for your services and promotes your business. So it isn't sales. Your website is a marketing tool just as a training courses and networking can be. Read on, it's important.

Why Is Marketing Important?

To help answer this question, let me give you a couple of examples.

Maria set up her consulting practice seven years ago. Already an acknowledged expert in her field with wide-ranging, high-level connections, she was picky about the projects she chose to work on, and she turned down as much work as she accepted. Always planning to work on her own, she employed an administrative assistant to field her calls, submit her invoices, maintain her website, and so on. Commanding a high fee rate and always with a work surplus, Maria reached an ideal position that few consultants will ever attain.

Julie left her job in middle management with an electric utility and set up her own consulting company four months ago. Though she managed to get a small amount of work from her old employer, she struggled to get anything else. While competent in her line of work, she wasn't well known, even in her field. Her main source of contacts was at the utility she used to work at, which of course was limited in both the scope and range of potential consulting work.

So, first question: are you a Maria or a Julie?

If you're a Maria, I'm amazed you're reading this book, and you can certainly skip this chapter on marketing, because you don't need to spend time on it. Work flows in the door for you, and obviously getting out there, developing marketing material, making new contacts isn't something you need to be concerned with. On the other hand, you may want to do a couple of speaking engagements now and again to keep your name at the forefront, but you probably do that anyway. Congratulations to you!

If you're a Julie, I hope this book will help you. One of your problems is that not many people know you, have heard of your company, recognize your range of capabilities, or know what benefit they may get from engaging you on a project. On this basis, even if they do stumble across you, you may be a risky proposition. From their perspective, why should they take a chance on you when they could use another consultant they've worked with before? This is a problem many consultants have, especially when they start out. In part, it's solved by a series of marketing actions.

Most likely you fall somewhere in the middle between Maria and Julie. For you, regular marketing actions are key to keeping your business moving forward, maintaining your presence in the marketplace, and developing your scope of services. If you refer to the typical breakdown of the consulting week in chapter 4, you'll see that 20 percent of your time should be spent on marketing. It's very easy to allow that to diminish to very little over time, which can cause major problems (unless you've become a Maria).

Please understand that marketing is very important—critical, in fact—to the success of a consulting business. Market too little at your peril, and remember that the limit of peril is different depending on the development of your business. Marketing is also difficult because it's general, and it's usually difficult to extrapolate a direct line between your marketing actions and your sales. This means that it's also possible to spend far too much time, effort, and money on marketing actions. It's ideal to maintain the balance on an ongoing basis in a way that works for you.

What Marketing Actions Should I Be Thinking About?

One of the difficulties with marketing is that there are so many potential actions out there—more than ever in the last few years with the explosion of online marketing. The actions that you should consider depend on the type, nature, maturity, and success of your business. I've listed a number of fairly generic marketing actions below, but consider these points as you review them:

- A balance of actions that works for your business is ideal.
- No marketing actions are free, so you need to develop a marketing budget and also add your time to your cost; it's not free either.
- Marketing has to be ongoing and evolving, so try to think ahead as you consider what may work for you.

Here are some marketing actions (in no particular order) you may consider:

- networking
- newsletters / e-mail marketing
- writing and publishing articles
- presenting / speaking
- training / teaching
- website
- pro-bono work
- referrals

- advertising
- membership in groups and associations
- listings with appropriate organizations
- positioning and posting on social media, such as Facebook, LinkedIn, and Twitter

You can probably think of a few more. The difficulty, of course, is choosing the ones that work best for you at this particular point in time.

How Do I Develop a Marketing Strategy?

Of course, your strategy depends on a variety of factors, not the least of which is where you are in the development of your business, what you've tried (if anything) in the past, how much money and time you have to assign to marketing, and so on. I've found it almost impossible to come up with a strategy by starting with the list of things I can do. It's best, in my opinion, to start at the other end.

What is a strategy but a means to an end? In this case, a marketing strategy is a means to develop a demand for your services and to promote your business. But it doesn't matter how well you're promoted or how much demand there is for your services; what really matters is how much business you get in the door. For example, you could pay a lot of money and have a sales booth at, say, an accounting conference. By the end of the event, your business may be very well promoted to the attendees at that conference. But if none of them is in a position to engage you on contract even if he wanted to, the net result of all that time and money will be zero return.

So think about what you want and which sectors you would like to work with. Okay, now think of anyone you know in that sector that you would like to get a sales meeting with. What marketing actions could you take that would increase the likelihood of getting in front of her? Obtaining a referral from someone you've already worked for who knows that person would be ideal. Going to or even speaking at an event that she is likely to attend could work very well. You could also send a short introductory e-mail and follow up with a call. Maybe you could connect with that person on LinkedIn.

Perhaps your targets are more general. For example, you want to get contracts in the food and beverage sectors, because that's where you have the best track record. Okay, you know the sectors, you know the people. What would be the best ways to promote yourself and your company to them?

Bear in mind as you prepare your strategy that all marketing takes time and costs money. You, like the rest of us, will be limited on both. So plan your marketing for the year. How much time and money are you going to assign? If you have one day a week and $5,000, tailor your actions accordingly.

Where Does a Website Fit In?

I know a young couple that started a business. Well, that's what they told me anyway, and I believed them. They had a good idea to provide some specific consulting services in a niche market. Nothing wrong with that.

I met up with them a couple of months later and asked them how things were going. "Still working on the website" was the answer I got. "But it should be up and running in a few weeks, and then we can start." All they did in the first four months of operation of the business was work on, refine, add to, and try to perfect the website.

In the meantime, they had no cash coming in and a lot going out to web designers, video producers, and the like. They spent somewhere in the region of $20,000 in the quest for the perfect website with the belief that business would flow in once it was launched. Unfortunately it didn't, and the business ended up costing them a lot of money and causing them a lot of personal hardship. The website looked great though.

It's a sad story and a cautionary one. The obvious lesson is this: don't let your website drive your consulting business. Certainly it has its place, but not at the expense of everything else.

So why do you want a website, and what do you want it to do for you?

First, a website is a marketing tool for your consulting business, not a sales tool. Yes, hopefully someone may discover your website and subsequently contact you, and that may lead to some work down the line. But it's extremely unlikely that a contract for work will float through to you just on the basis of someone seeing your website. If that has happened to you, congratulations. Please send me your contact details so I can look at your website.

Most of the time, your website will be used to assure somebody that you're competent and professional. It's a backup. If I've just met you at a seminar and I'm interested in finding more about you and your company, I'll go to your website. And I'll probably do that before I send you an e-mail or give you a call. So with that premise in mind, you need a website that satisfies that need. And you need to allocate time and money to your website in accordance with its place in your overall marketing strategy.

People have different opinions about what they want on their website, the look and feel of it, the amount of detail, and so on. It's your consulting company, and it should reflect you and your business—and to an extent, your personality. So it's very difficult in a book like this to advise specifically on how your website should look and how it should target your market. However, for what it's worth, here are my two cents on what your website should contain:

- a clear statement of your business goals and objectives
- a clear statement of the services you can provide
- some details of your track record
- key points that differentiate you and your business
- some referrals
- some details about you and your staff, if you have any, including some personal details

- very clear and easy contact details
- a blog
- an item that can be downloaded, such as an article you've written or an ebook

Those last couple of items will improve the visibility of your website on search engines. And I can almost guarantee that as soon as you launch your website, you'll start to receive e-mails advertising search engine optimization (SEO). Personally, I haven't followed up on any of them, but to each his own.

How Much Time and Money Do I Devote to Marketing?

Remember the first part of this chapter, with Maria and Julia? If you're Maria, you can afford plenty of marketing. If you're Julia, you can't afford much. But how much can you afford? And can you afford not to spend very much?

Let's look at time first. As already stated multiple times, you need to make sure your forward-load pipeline has enough in it to keep you going. That means you have to be proposing work to potential clients and subsequently converting the proposals into work. When you're starting out, you have to find the potential clients in the first place, and your marketing actions make that happen. Of course, there are a multitude of potential actions you can take—and they'll all take up your time.

So here's a rule of thumb: spend around 20 percent of your time marketing (one day per week if you work full time) when you're in the first five years of your consulting business. After that, hopefully you're moving more toward Maria than Julia, so you may be able to ease off. And choose the marketing actions that you think will work well for you. Inevitably, some of those will work well, and some won't. So it's a case of trial and error for most of us.

Okay, so I've allocated my day per week, but how much money do I spend? Bear in mind that every dollar you spend on marketing is one dollar off your profit margin. Well, how about this for a rule of thumb? You made a business plan, right? Well, sort of anyway. Okay, so how much did you expect to make on an annual basis after you've paid out for all your other expenses, like office rent, software, travel costs, and so forth? $200,000? Good for you! Well, if you're allocating 20 percent of your time, allocate 10 percent of your profit. And see how it goes.

As you've probably guessed, this is a difficult area, and you might be rolling your eyes right now. Or you're thinking I've recommended way too little. But others will think I've recommended way too much. Of course it depends where you are with your business but also what consulting business you're in. Some require much more in the way of corporate marketing, wining and dining, attendance at trade shows, and so on, than others. You know your business, and if your clients expect bottles of champagne and box seats at the hockey game, a budget of 10 percent probably won't cut it. It's only a guideline.

How Do I Know If It's Working and If It's Enough?

Have you ever heard the saying "If you can't measure it, you can't manage it"? If you don't keep records of what you're spending and when, you never know how much money is in your account. Obvious and boring, I know. A business generally accounts for all its incomings and outgoings with a high degree of accuracy. And part of that accounting is the marketing budget, which may be broken down into a bunch of separate activities: trade shows, seminars, website, entertaining, and the like. But that's almost always where it stops. No one takes the time to assess what the $4,562 spent on trade show attendance led to in terms of benefit.

Half the problem lies in defining what the benefit is. There's certainly benefit in being present at a trade show; it gets your company name out there, reinforces that you're a player in the market, reminds people that you're providing services in that sector, and so on. All those things are good, but they're intangible. If that's the extent of it, you can't put a value on it. On the other hand, if Mr. X came up to you at the event and ended up engaging you for a project, that's a direct benefit you can assign to your attendance at that show.

So let's accept that you can't quantify everything. That doesn't mean that trying to measure it is a waste of time. And quantifying your time is easy.

So keep track of what you spend and the time you commit to marketing efforts. And track any direct benefits you can assign to your efforts. If you met someone at a seminar you presented at, and it led to a project, going to that seminar was certainly worthwhile. You can assign value to that, and you will probably decide to attend the next seminar of that type.

If you've attended a trade show three years in succession and never got any work that you can directly assign to that effort, perhaps you need to evaluate whether it's worth going in year four. As stated earlier, not all your marketing activities will bear fruit, so it's best to have at least the basis for some form of evaluation.

This sort of ongoing analysis tells you, to some degree, whether or not your time and money committed has been worthwhile. As a result, it gives you input as to whether to change your marketing package or stick with the current plan. But it doesn't tell you whether it's enough—or too much.

It's certainly possible to spend too much time and money on marketing; remember my example of the young couple with the fantastic website. It's also easy to commit too little to it and suffer as a result. The only way you know whether or not it's enough is to continually assess and review your business—something that you're probably doing anyway. If you're happy with the way things are going overall, if you have enough work and enough in the pipeline, then chances are that your marketing mix is working well for you. If, unhappily, you're not in such a joyful position, maybe you aren't doing enough on the marketing front. Or perhaps what you're doing is yielding little benefit. Either way, you need to change it up.

One final point: Don't beat yourself up if you're struggling in this area. I don't think anyone gets it completely right; if they do, they aren't aware of it, because much of it is impossible to measure. Also, things are changing all the time. Think of the rise of social media in the last ten years. Where will we be in another ten?

CHAPTER 6

Getting the Work

I don't think this will come as a great revelation to anyone who has read this far in the book, but if you can't get any work, you don't have a consulting business. Also—minor point—you don't have any money coming in. Okay, not that minor. And, really, it's not just some work you need; it's a steady, life-sustaining stream, ideally without long dry periods between periods of manic activity.

In my discussions with people who are thinking of becoming consultants, the question of where the work comes from is usually one of the first, if not the very first, they ask. That's not surprising, for reasons already stated above. In fact, the potential for work is all around you. It's just a case of being able to first identify it and then to get ahold of it. So let me explain.

Where Does the Work Come From?

There are many sources of work, and they're all around you as well as further afield. Consider the following:

- referrals from companies you previously conducted consulting work for
- companies that you already completed consulting work for
- ex-employers

- companies or consultants you worked with when you were an employee
- colleagues from previous companies you worked at
- companies in your field of expertise
- consulting companies that work in your field
- contacts from speaking engagements
- contacts from marketing actions you've taken
- contacts through publications you've written
- contacts through placing yourself on lists
- organizations' requests for proposals
- contacts you meet at seminars and networking events

This is by no means an exhaustive list, but it's certainly enough to go with for now. If you live in or near a city, there's probably enough work in and around that city to keep you busy. This means you get the choice whether or not to travel.

Yet there is less and less need for travel. A couple of years ago, I completed a package of work for an ex-colleague now based in Sydney, Australia. Everything was accomplished electronically with no need to travel—which was unfortunate in this case, as I would have enjoyed an expenses-paid trip to Sydney. Much can be accomplished worldwide while you sit in your pajamas with your iPad.

How Do I Know Where to Look for Work?

Take a bit of time, go somewhere quiet, sit peacefully with your coffee, and write down some answers to these questions:

- What is my skill set, and where does my main body of experience lie?
- Where has my work come from so far?
- Who do I know who works in my field?
- Who do I know who knows people in my field?
- What other consultants do I know in my field?
- Who would be my ideal client?

- Which seminars and events would my ideal client go to?
- What organizations should I join to improve my chances of getting work?
- What would be my ideal consulting project?

If you're just starting out, the second question above is difficult to answer from a consulting perspective. So think back to work you did while you were employed, but think about how you would have approached it if you were a consultant doing it—or perhaps doing select parts of it. And that's a good question in itself: if you had to contract parts of it out, which parts would you choose?

In my experience, the best sources of work are the following:

- Clients who you've already worked for, ideally in large companies; they know you, you know them. It's easy to approach them with some other idea for work or ask them for contacts to do similar work at another location.
- Other consultants. They are often overlooked as a source of work, especially if you view consulting work from a scarcity point of view. If yours is a scarcity viewpoint, other consultants are competitors, so why would you work with them? If yours is an abundance viewpoint, there's more than enough work for everyone, so why wouldn't you work with them? Let me be bold enough to suggest that if you have the scarcity viewpoint, get off your high horse and change your outlook.
- Ex-employers. Unless you left under a cloud (did you really say that to your boss?), ex-employers are generally good sources of future consulting work. If you've just left to start your own consulting business, they may well be the best source at this time.

What Types of Clients Are There?

There are lots and lots of client types, obviously, and the whole range of personalities. But when you view them from a consulting perspective, they tend to fall into categories based on the businesses they work in. Obviously there are exceptions to the rule, but generally they fit into the following categories:

Government (federal, provincial, state, local)

These can provide a steady stream of work once you're a trusted consultant. And generally that work isn't rushed and is well specified. On the other hand, they tend to have very strict rules that require them to obtain competitive quotes for even low-value work packages. Strangely, these rules seem to melt away toward the end of the financial year, when the budget has to be spent or it's cut back for the next year. So being in the right place at the right time can pay dividends. The "rules" can also make these jobs time consuming, as they may require frequent meetings and progress reports. They also can be very picky about the final product. There's also the advantage—or disadvantage, depending how you view it—that they pay on a strict predetermined schedule.

Public or part publicly owned organizations (utilities, state or provincial insurance companies, etc.)

Most of the same points above apply, but I've found that generally the rules aren't as strict as those in government project, and they tend to be less demanding in terms of meetings and updates. Work is generally not too pressured, and I find these organizations generally good to work for. Like governments, they pay on a predetermined schedule, so you know when you'll get your money, and it may not be as soon as you'd like.

Private organizations

Depending on who they are, they're likely to be a lot less rule driven. So perhaps you can cut a good deal, get paid quickly or even in advance, and not need to be in competition because a rule says that anything over $5,000 has to go out for three or more quotations (avoid, avoid, avoid). You get the chance to be much more entrepreneurial, follow up work directly, and generally get higher fees. However, your work may be subject to much more time pressure, and you may find yourself dealing with scope creep (your project is extended with no extra payment for you; see chapter 9).

Consulting companies

For a small consulting company, there are lots of advantages in partnering with or subcontracting to larger consulting companies:

- You can end up working for major organizations that are unlikely to have engaged you directly.
- They likely have client contacts at a higher level than you do.
- If there's a proposal to be written, they'll do most of it.
- You can charge higher fees to fit in with their fee structure.
- If you fill a niche for them, it's easy to become their go-to consultant for certain projects.
- They'll do most of the basic organization on the project, including the preparation of invoices and other administrative tasks.
- The other side of the coin is that you probably won't be paid until they do, so you're dependent on their collection system, which may be slow.

There are pros and cons to working with all these types of clients, and which sectors you're happy with depends on you and your business.

I Can't Sell ... Can I?

Simple answer: Yes. Yes, you can.

I've lost count of the number of times in my career that I've heard the words "I can't sell" or "I'm not a salesman" or "I don't know how to sell." It's very common, and it's a misconception in the vast majority of cases. But as we know, in effect, perception is reality; if you say or even think that you can't sell, you can't.

Part of the problem stems from what we envisage when someone says the word *sales* or *salesperson* to us. Maybe we think of someone who's very outgoing, very pushy, very persuasive. And we think, *That's not me.* I've been consulting successfully for many years, and that's not me either.

Years ago, I was employed by a large brewing and retail organization and was asked to purchase some optical equipment for a research project. After reviewing what was available, I selected some products and contacted the sales department to get someone to run through the products with me. I was happy with what I'd read and seen, but I wanted a couple of small points explained before I placed an order. In other words, I was ready to buy.

The company's representative arrived and immediately launched into a sales pitch that I couldn't stop. He wouldn't listen to me and refused to take the time to understand what I wanted. By the end of it, he had turned me off so completely that I wouldn't have taken his products if he'd given them to me for free.

That representative misread me and my situation entirely. As I've said before, putting yourself in the clients' shoes is the key to successful consulting. It's also the key to *selling* consulting. You aren't selling door-to-door, and you aren't cold calling. You're generally dealing with someone like you: someone who likes to be listened to, respected, and not pushed into something.

If you've ever persuaded anyone to do anything, you can sell. For that's what selling is. In our business, it's persuading others that you can do work for them that will benefit them in some way. That may be done in a written proposal, where you get time to think about it, lay it all out, and consider what points would work to best effect. If you're face-to-face with someone, you're probably just discussing the problem or issue. Perhaps you're explaining the type of work you've already done; this is easy, because you know it so well. Overall, you're trying to get along with that potential client, because most consulting is sold because the clients like who they're dealing with. Obviously they need to have confidence that you can do the work as well, but they aren't generally going to give work to someone they dislike, irrespective of how good that person appears to be.

Think about times when you've bought something and been at your most comfortable. (I'd be willing to bet that wasn't at a car dealership.) What did he or she say or do that made you comfortable and relaxed, and got you to agree to buy whatever it was? Probably that salesperson was pleasant without being over familiar, listened to you, answered your questions, quietly promoted the product by telling you what was good about it, and let you take your time coming to your decision. And I'm pretty sure you could do the same, couldn't you?

So here's a suggestion. Next time you're going to meet with someone who might want you to do some consulting work, don't think of it as a sales opportunity. Think of it as a discussion. Before your discussion, write down a few points you want to bring up. Get the other person to talk about the need, problem, or whatever it is, and listen to what she has to say. By all means, make some suggestions as to what might help, but don't interrupt.

Near the end of the meeting, try to paraphrase the problem or need. For example, "I just want to make sure I understand ..." Then at some point say, "How about I go away and put a few ideas down in the form of a proposal for you to consider?" Unless you goofed up badly at some point, in which case you probably know already, most people say yes to that question.

Undoubtedly the more experience you have at this, the better you get. But there's only one way to get the experience: by going out and trying. But eliminate the word *sales* from your mind to take the pressure off yourself.

One last point: If you're short of work and desperately want some more, try to get that out of your mind when you go in to meet a potential client. If that's how you feel, it always shows, and you won't succeed. Tell yourself that if nothing comes of this meeting, it really doesn't matter. That's not so easy to do, but it makes a big difference.

So you can sell. Of course you can sell. You're just not going to call it that or think of it that way.

What Do I Actually Do to Get Work?

If you've been a consultant for a while, I hope you've already figured out what you need to do, but perhaps a refresher wouldn't hurt. If you're just starting out, this is for you.

As with most things in any profession, there aren't any hard-and-fast rules, and there are lots of ways that work may come to you. Here are the most common ways:

- Customer enquiry. Someone calls you or e-mails you and says, "Hey, I'm looking for some assistance with a new project we have underway."
- Customer meeting. You get in touch with someone, perhaps as a result of bumping into him at a seminar, perhaps calling because you haven't caught up with her for a while. As a result of the discussion that follows, however it happens, you identify the potential to help this client with something—and you're off to the races.
- Request for Proposal (RFP). You respond to an RFP issued by an organization.

There are many variations, but most ways of getting work are covered in the three points above. However, this is only half the story (actually way less than half). Just because you've talked to someone about potential work doesn't mean it's going to happen. If Laura, your potential client, says, "Hey, I'm looking for some assistance with a new project we have underway," from that point on, there's a lot that you both need to agree on. What the project is, how much work she's looking for, what she's prepared to pay, when you're going to start, plus a number of other things, need to be sorted out. And this is where the proposal comes in.

The next section covers proposals in some detail. But, in essence, a proposal is a written document that you prepare that covers all the points I just mentioned. And that's not the end of the story. Often there will be some to-ing and fro-ing on some points in the proposal until you're both (reasonably) happy. Then, once you have agreement, you need that formalized. Ideally you'll get a purchase order; at minimum you'll get an e-mail instructing you to proceed or a signature on the back page of your proposal. Until you get to that point, you don't have the work.

Here's a cautionary tale: A government client of mine, who I'd worked for on a number of projects over a couple of years, contacted me. She asked me for a proposal for a package of work that we discussed over the phone. I duly responded and followed up. After sorting out a couple of minor points, we reached an agreement. She said she'd send through a purchase order and was adamant that I start on Monday—in ten days.

The next few days passed, and the purchase order didn't arrive. I nudged her a couple of times by e-mail, and both times she said it would be sent through. I called her on the Thursday before the project was to start, and she confirmed that everything was okay and that I'd get the PO later that day or first thing Friday. So a start on Monday was still the plan.

On Friday afternoon she called me to say the project was canceled and that she was sorry. Her department was involved in some sort of government scandal, and all ongoing work had been suspended. I never did get that work, as she left the government a few months later and, believe it or not, set up her own consulting business.

So the moral of this story is "It's never over till it's over." Get the purchase order and then celebrate, not before.

What Is a Proposal?

At its simplest, a proposal is a price quotation, usually written but sometimes verbal, such as "I will do that work for ten thousand dollars."

However, in practice, usually more is required. You need more in your proposal so that both you and the client are clear on what's going to be done, when, and for how much.

A brief step back: A proposal should be a confirmation of an agreement; a statement of how you and the client are going to work together *in partnership.* Yes, they are your clients, and yes, they're paying you, but you're nearly always dependent on them for some information, access to staff, key details, or something. It's in their interests to help you do the best job possible, because the work is helping them. Otherwise, why did they engage you in the first place? So it should always be a partnership.

Also, your client shouldn't be surprised by your proposal. If they have budgeted $10,000 for the work and you quote $50,000 in your proposal, you're not exactly singing off the same hymn sheet (to use an old British expression).

So let's think about what you and your client need to confirm in the proposal, bearing in mind that someone who hasn't been party to your discussions, like your contact's boss, may read it. Generally the following are needed:

- a *brief* introduction to you and your company
- an overview of the work, what issue you're helping with, problem you're addressing, what value you're bringing
- information on who is going to work on the project - you may want to attach résumés if it's a new client
- details as to what you will be doing—generally a list of action steps
- deliverables—what you will provide
- a timescale—when you will start and finish, and what will be delivered when
- fees and expenses details
- invoicing details—what your invoicing schedule is
- an agreement / signoff

Often other points will need to be confirmed. For example, sometimes the client will need to provide some information by a certain date. You need to set out what will happen if this doesn't occur. Are you still going to carry on? Will you invoice the full amount? As usual, put yourself in the client's shoes and think what he needs to agree to.

In general, proposals should be short, clear, and to the point. You can't and shouldn't try to cover every item in a proposal. Describing what you'll do has to be covered in broad points, as you can't cover every possible eventuality. Another very good reason to keep your proposal short is that no one has time to read long documents these days. I'm sure you don't want to write them, and your clients don't want to read them. So keep your proposals concise.

The exception to the "keep it concise rule" is when you respond to an RFP. Although the rule still applies to a degree, often RFPs ask for so much information that you end up with a big document. And then they'll demand four bound hard copies, so you need to go to all the expense of printing, binding, and couriering. (Why, why, why in this day and age?) But RFPs are a whole subject of their own.

What's a USP?

The acronym USP is consultant jargon for Unique Selling Point. Don't you just love jargon? No? I hate it. So now you know what USP stands for, what does it actually mean? Well, in basic English, or as near as I can get, it means the key thing that differentiates you from the rest of pack and will make sure you get the project. Any wiser? Let me give you an example.

I once was involved in a project in Estonia, working for the European Commission. Estonia is the northernmost of the Baltic States, squeezed between Finland to the west and Russia to the east—in case you like this geographical stuff. It's a fascinating, beautiful place that I'd recommend to anybody, but I digress. Part of the project, as defined by the Commission, was to find an engineer who was resident in Western Europe but spoke English and Estonian and had the requisite consulting skills to work on the project. I remember someone joking sarcastically at the meeting that there wouldn't be any trouble satisfying that requirement.

Back home we started putting out a few feelers and stumbled across Tony. A sophisticated, well-qualified, highly experienced engineer and resident of Dublin, Ireland, Tony was Estonian by birth and fluent in the language. He also happened to be an independent consultant with gaps in his schedule to allow him to work in Estonia. In terms of USPs, Tony had them all. How could we not hire him?

Tony is probably an extreme example. For most of us, a USP is not really unique, but a good, relevant selling point. For example, if you're chasing a project with a major hotel chain, and you've already successfully completed similar assignments with Hilton, Holiday Inn, and Radisson, you're in a very good position to get the work. Not many, if any, of the consulting companies you are in competition with will be able to point to that level of experience. I'd regard that as a USP.

Really, a USP is the thing that makes you stand out from the rest. If you can complete a sentence that starts "What makes us different is …" or "What makes us ideally suited for this work is …" you're defining your USP(s).

USPs need to be marketed, because they're a major selling point (by definition). Nobody knows about them unless you tell them. It's good to have them clearly emphasized on your website, but it's not enough to do only that. They need to be emphasized regularly to your key clients and in your proposals and discussions on potential work. They also need to be built upon as your experience grows. For example, if your hotel experience now includes Hyatt as well, you need to get the word out there.

How Do I Work Out the Cost I'm Proposing to Charge?

If you read the earlier section on proposals, you may have noticed that I wrote about fees and expenses but not about fee rates. Many consultants use a fee rate to work out how much they will charge. It's simple that way: my rate is $150 per hour; I think it will take me one hundred hours, so I'll charge $15,000.

In many respects, there isn't much wrong with this. Presumably you've done the sums and worked out that if you're working on projects for a certain number of hours per week at $150 per hour, you make a wage you're happy with. Many people charge this way—lawyers, for example (but never as low as $150 per hour, in my experience).

Look at this from another perspective, and you might determine that there's a lot wrong with this way of charging. One big issue is that it takes no account of *the value you're providing.*

Take the example above where you've worked out a charge of $15,000 for the work. Suppose the company benefits to the tune of $1 million from your input. It would have undoubtedly been prepared to pay a lot more than you charged. In this case, the value provided compared to the fee is huge. The company would probably have been happy to pay at least $100,000, maybe $200,000. And from their perspective, they don't care how many hours you put in. You saved them $1 million, end of story.

Okay, this is an extreme example, but you get the point. Consider the value of what you're providing. Often this is difficult to work out, but make an estimate if you can. At least then you get some more perspective on what you're proposing, and you can set that in context in your proposal. And charging 10 percent of the value you're providing is usually acceptable.

The second issue is the client you're working for. I once did some work for a partner at one of the Big Four accounting companies. Her fee rate, she confessed to me once, was $975 per hour. So for a company like that, paying $20,000 to a consultant is a bit of loose change. You can charge that company a lot more than a smaller operation. Actually it comes back to value again, because what you're offering is probably worth more in a big company, simply because it's bigger.

There are other issues to take into account. Are you in competition with another consultant? Have you worked for the company before? Is it worth taking a financial hit on this job to get in the door with a desired client? Do you actually want to do this work? Are there other complications that will cause you stress, such as a very short timeframe for completion? If you have to travel, are they prepared to pay for your travel time? Are they going to pay up front, or will you have to wait three months for your money?

What it comes down to is that each project has to be separately evaluated, so please don't work out a fee rate for yourself and stick to it like it's carved in stone. You may end up charging two clients different amounts for exactly the same work—and that's fine. The value you provide will be different in each case.

Working out what to charge is something you get better at the more experience you have. It's essential to track your hours on projects so that you know what you're actually earning and to direct you to where the more profitable business lies in the future. If you work out that some of your projects have paid you $100 per hour while some brought in $250 per hour, that really should tell you something.

One last point: There is a tendency among consultants, particularly newly minted ones, to underrate themselves. You're a valuable resource for a company, so don't be shy about charging accordingly.

How Do I Decide How Long It Will Take?

I once worked with someone who was an excellent consultant in most respects. He always delivered good work on time, got on well with clients, and so forth. However, his one big failing was timekeeping. He was unable to complete a project in anything like the number of hours allotted for it. Eventually he lost his job with the consulting company he worked for because of it. For a company that runs on number of hours booked at certain fee rates, booking one hundred hours to a job that was allocated sixty doesn't go down well. He now runs his own consulting business, and I dread to think what his profit margin is. However, he's much happier now; he can take as many hours as he likes on each project.

I'll make no bones about it: working out how long a task will take is difficult. Think about doing a maintenance job at home. "This should take half an hour," you say to yourself, full of prejob enthusiasm. Two hours later, when all the screw heads are stripped, you've cut your thumb, and however hard you try, the water keeps leaking onto the floor. And you realize you may have been a tad optimistic.

So the first rule when you're working out how long a consulting project will take you is *be realistic*. Nothing ever takes five minutes, however small an action. Allocate at least half an hour.

Break down the project into as many little bits as you can, and assign a time to each of them. Think about what can go wrong, and make some allowances. If the project spreads over a period of weeks or months, you need to allocate time to get back up the learning curve again. Do you have to push the client to get information for you? Do you need to attend a lot of meetings? Do you need to travel far? All these things take time, and you should budget for them.

Okay, you've done that. Add it all up. Two hundred hours? Then allocate 240 hours. There's always stuff you can't account for and haven't or couldn't ever have thought of. If these things don't happen, and you do it quicker than you thought, great. Your effective hourly rate has gone up, and you've got spare time to do other things, like additional marketing or lazing by the pool—depending on how you're feeling.

A cautionary note: It's easy to become a slave to your own numbers. You've reached the end of the job, and you're about to submit the final report. You total up the time it actually took you, and you realize you spent only 190 hours. So instead of feeling happy and pressing "Send," you hear a nagging little voice inside ask, "Is it okay? Are you sure it's detailed enough? You've got fifty hours left in the budget."

Before you know it, you're going back over it, adding bits, checking, embellishing. In fact, all you're doing is spending the extra hours, which, let's face it, were the result of a lot of estimating in the first place. If you find yourself doing that, my advice is to stop. You thought it was good enough after 190 hours, and it was. Go sit by the pool!

Should I Work for Free, Just to Get Started?

Want the short answer? No! No, you shouldn't work for free. Definitely not. Well, only in one circumstance, which I'll explain later.

But what if you're just starting out and haven't got any track record? Surely if you go to XYZ Company and offer to work for free, you'll get a track record. Hopefully they'll be pleased with what you do, and then you can sell them some work. Doesn't that sound like a good idea?

No, it isn't a good idea. Don't do it. Don't even be tempted. Don't even think about it. It's the ultimate undervaluing of your service. It bypasses the whole reason that you're in the consulting industry, which is to perform a valuable service for commensurate fees.

You're just starting out, and I know it isn't easy. But how easy will it be to say to the company you've been working with for free, "Okay, now I'm going to charge you $200 per hour." Unless they're so ecstatic about what you've done that they can't get enough of you, it's going to be very difficult. Also, put yourself in their shoes. How much are you going to trust someone who's offering to work for free? If they take you on, it's likely to be on a low-level project that won't look good on your résumé.

Think of it from another angle. Try asking the guy painting your house to do the first room for free, and then you'll appraise it and consider paying him for the next room. Extend that analogy to your garage or your dentist. See what I mean?

Hopefully you got that message loud and clear, so what is the exception I mentioned at the start of this section? It's when you're doing pro bono work, probably for a charitable organization or some similar good cause. Even then you should value the work you do to the extent of invoicing them for that amount but nullifying it at the bottom of the invoice. It helps keep the books—and you—straight.

Do I Need a Purchase Order Before I Start?

Don't start work until you get one of the following:

- a purchase order (PO)
- a PO number, if not the order itself
- a signature on the sign-off sheet on your proposal or some other relevant document
- an e-mail instructing you to proceed

Most of the time you'll need one of the above to protect yourself, particularly if you're working with a new client, or a startup or small organization, or, dare I say it, a company you don't trust. Of course, if you don't trust them, why would you work for them anyway? But that's another matter.

The risk is that you go ahead and start working, commit time and expense, and don't get paid when you submit an invoice. The client says that there was no contract, no PO—in fact, no project. It's a bad situation all around that I'm sure we all want to avoid.

When you consult for an organization, you're entering into a professional arrangement with them and a partnership. It's no more than professional to ask for one of the four items detailed above, preferably a PO. If your clients don't want to commit to any of these, they aren't being professional. And that should be a big red flag. My advice is to dig your heels in and say that you won't start until you get a commitment proved by one of these. If they still won't, walk away; you've probably had a lucky escape.

You don't always need a PO or equivalent. Perhaps you've been working with a client for years and have a great relationship. She calls you up because she needs some help *now,* and you start working for her in a couple of days. You know she'll pay you, so you don't need any more commitment from her. It's down to trust, or lack of it, at the end of the day.

Another instance can occur when you're working for clients from a different culture. A friend of mine told me about some work he was doing for a foreign client that was all agreed on a handshake. He was advised that it would be a great insult to demand any further evidence of commitment, so he didn't. He has now been working with them for more than two years, and they pay every one of his invoices within two weeks of receiving them.

So you don't need a PO or equivalent *all* the time. But most of the time you do. In Western culture, I think it's a reasonable professional expectation for you to ask (if commitment is not forthcoming) and for your client to comply.

What About a Contract? I Want to Get Paid, Not Sued!

No one wants lawsuits. Some consultants are good; some aren't so good. But not one that I've known has ever had legal action taken against him by a client. So, first of all, let's get this in perspective. Being sued is something that rarely happens to consultants.

If you're a client, and you're extremely unhappy with what your consultant has provided, what are you going to do? Well, most likely you're going to refuse to pay. If you've already paid, you may demand a refund and threaten legal action. And, of course, you're never going to use that consultant again. But are you going to embroil your company in a legal battle? Probably not.

Of course, there are exceptions to this. If, for example, you're an engineering consultant, your heating system design was fundamentally flawed, and no one noticed before it was built. Then there will certainly be some serious comeback. But this is why engineers have professional indemnity insurance.

Okay, so you need insurance. We talked about that back in chapters 2 and 3. Find out what your peers have, talk to insurance companies, and get yourself covered.

All that is well and good, but I remember being very concerned about this issue when I started consulting. The thing that concerned me, and I believe it concerns many consultants, is that the job isn't totally *specified*. For example, if you're contracted to carry out a study on some aspects of a company's business, it's probably based on a proposal you wrote. And consulting proposals generally aren't detailed specifications.

A good example of this is a project I carried out for a large utility a couple of years ago. Their affiliated business competed within the private sector, supplying energy services for large new developments. A director I know well asked me to research what competition was out there for their new business and to present the findings at a meeting of their senior management in six weeks. I asked him what they were looking to spend on the project and prepared a two-page proposal for that amount.

So how much time do you spend on a project like that? How much research do you do? The fact is that you could spend months researching every potential company that might impact business, but of course you're not going to do that. You're going to put yourself in the director's shoes and say to yourself, "If I was paying him X dollars to do that work, what would I expect him to cover?" And that's what you're going to do.

You could worry about being very exposed taking on a job like that. After all, you could always be accused of not going deep enough with the research and be threatened with legal action if you don't do a lot more work—and a lot more besides. It's never happened to me, and I've never heard of it happening. Just keep the client informed as you go along, maintain a good working relationship, and it won't be a problem.

So don't waste time and energy worrying about being sued. Remember that consulting should be a partnership between you and your client, and partners are supposed to get along, not take legal action against each other. (I hope you didn't just get divorced.) Concentrate on doing a professional job that you're proud of and would be happy to receive if you were the client, and I don't think you can go too far wrong.

I've Finished. How Do I Get the Next Job?

Hopefully you never need to ask yourself or anyone else this question. In an ideal consulting world, you'll have a few jobs on the go and a few more potential jobs in the pipeline. Having said that, the ideal world isn't always where we're working, and things don't always go according to plan. If you've just started out in consulting, sold your first piece of work, dived into it with enthusiasm, and now you're out the other side, this may be the situation you find yourself in. Hindsight is a wonderful thing, but here's what you should have done:

- However enticing, exciting, enthralling, or simply pressurized that project was, you shouldn't have worked on it full time. You should always—I mean always—be looking to keep the job pipeline flowing. That means taking time to undertake marketing actions, follow up on leads, visit potential clients, and so forth. Even if none of these actions result in work, at least you have some potential work when you finish your current project.

- When you were working with the last client, you probably met a few people in the organization and got a good understanding of their business. You should have taken the time to speak with key people about their jobs, their problems, where the company is headed, and so on, with a view to selling them some more work at a later date. After all, they know you, and hopefully they're happy with you and feel you did a good job. It's much easier for them to give you another contract than someone they don't know. And you'd be happy to do more work for them, wouldn't you?

- Back to that client again. You should have asked for a referral. What do I mean by a referral? Someone the client knows who may have a need for the services you provide. That may be someone in another organization or someone in another part of the same company. A referral is a valuable thing to have and a great way to get more work. Don't be scared to ask; I know I was when I started out. It's a perfectly fair, reasonable, professional question, and I've never had a client who has been offended by it—in fact, mainly they're pleased to help if they can.

So if you didn't do any of these things and have fallen off the proverbial cliff, you now know what you should have done. If you didn't speak to those key people in the organization, do it now. And follow up with that VP and ask for a referral now? Then pick up all those actions that you should have taken time out to cover while you were working for Acme Enterprises or whoever they were. And have faith; you sold that job, you can sell another. In fact, it's easier now.

Is It Better to Concentrate on My Old Customers or to Try to Get New Ones?

If you consider this question in probability terms, the answer is that it's better to concentrate on your old customers. Depending on what you read, who you listen to, and who the latest business guru is, it's seven to ten times easier to get more work from an existing client than to find a new client who wants to work with you. The reasons are all obvious. With your existing clients

- you have a track record;
- you know their business;
- they know you as reliable, competent, and professional (right?); and
- you have a number of good contacts you can talk to.

So follow the guru's advice and chase up your old clients.

All well and good, but suppose you're just starting out and you have only one or two clients? Follow the guru religiously, and you'll never have more than one or two clients. And there has to be a time when any client is a new client. And who are these gurus anyway?

So the answer is that it depends where you are in your consulting business development and what your current situation is. If you're well established with a lengthy track record yet you're a bit short of work, absolutely follow up with some past clients. The chances of solving the temporary gap in the pipeline are good.

On the other hand, if you're looking to grow your business, you'll need more clients. So focus your marketing actions on your sector of choice or on following up with existing clients to get referrals for potential new clients.

In practice, it's not an either / or question. You should be doing both. It's good business practice to keep in regular contact with your existing clients. The probabilities tell you that. Look ahead a year, and I'm sure you'd like to have at least a couple of new clients, so do something to attract them. However, it's definitely not easy to get new clients. The time and effort to do this requires that you undertake it when your business is going well, not when you're short of work and starting to worry about the mortgage payment.

Another important point is the boredom factor. For example, Mark, a friend of mine, worked for an insurance company from the age of twenty until he retired. He ended up in middle management and, as I recall, never once has complained about his job (probably a record of some sort). He is witty, engaging, and excellent company. And although we get along great, we're very different in our outlook on work. I could never do the job he does; I simply get bored too easily and need variety. That's why I'm a consultant and, I suspect, why a lot of us end up in this profession.

So you become a consultant, and you aren't bored. But still the grass is greener on the other side. In short, there's a temptation to spend lots of time chasing new clients because it's fun and you think that those clients may be more exciting than the bunch of current clients you have. And before you know it, you're neglecting your existing clients and your forward load pipeline is a bit thin. So try to rein yourself in, just a bit.

How Do I Decide Whether or Not to Respond to Requests for Proposals (RFPs)?

Here are a couple of scenarios to set the scene:

- Business is going well. You're working for a couple of clients, and in a week or two another project is due to kick off. And of course you're allocating time to bringing in future business. Then an RFP from a large government organization appears in your in-box. Intrigued by the title, you read all fifty-six pages of it and feel it's tailor-made for you. The deadline is in three weeks, so you stop what you're doing and spend much of the next three weeks sorting out partners, agreeing on fee rates, working out hours, and writing what turns out to be a large document. You pay for four bound copies as specified and a courier to make sure it gets there on time. Three weeks later, you're told you've made the final three and are asked to give a presentation on a certain day. More work, but you're encouraged to have gotten this far. You put in the time and effort to make the presentation really slick. You and your partners do a good job but end up coming in second. Despite a follow-up feedback session, you never really find out why.
- Same scenario, but you do a little research online and find out that twenty-three consulting organizations have downloaded the RFP. Not liking those odds, even though you think you have all the qualifications required, you choose to pass this time.
- You've been unsuccessful with the last six RFPs you submitted, and you think the problem is mainly cost. This time you price extremely competitively and are successful (at last). So you do the work, and when it's over you do some evaluation and realize you worked at 65 percent of your normal fee rate.

As you might have gathered, I have a few problems with RFPs. In short, I've wasted far too much time in my career responding to RFPs, so now I rarely even consider them. They're not an efficient way to win consulting work, for the following reasons:

- You never know if the playing field is even or not. Many organizations have internal rules that compel them to issue an RFP for a project above a certain value, often as low as $10,000. Particularly for the smaller jobs, the issuer may already have a preferred company in mind, and the RFP is just an exercise to comply with the rules. Numerous other factors can make the field uneven, and it's very hard to know if you have any chance at all.
- The odds aren't good. Typically you may be competing with ten other companies, often more. Okay, they may not all have your skill sets, but they may have some angle you don't have. Again, you just never know.
- Sometimes a company is desperate for work and will "buy" the project—that is, they'll lowball their offer just so they have some cash coming in and something on the company résumé.
- An RFP appears when it appears, coupled with a deadline. It forces you to find the time you need to complete it in a specific period, which often necessitates delaying fee-paying work or marketing actions.

You must make up your own mind regarding each RFP that comes out, but you probably have the gist of my feelings about them from the last few paragraphs. However, there's an exception to the rule of being extremely selective. If another (preferably larger) consulting company asks you to subcontract for them on an RFP submission, I recommend that you agree. This means that the other company does all the heavy lifting in terms of preparing the RFP, and probably all you need to do is submit a résumé and a small amount of script. I once obtained $50,000 of work in this way for an effort on the RFP that took me less than two hours. Now, those are the sort of odds I like.

Do I Want to Look for Work in Other Countries?

Consider these two scenarios. They both happened to me.

- Through a convoluted series of events, I ended up being flown to Siberia on a project paid for by the European Commission. The assignment was to run a practical training course to teach Russian engineers how to make their factories more energy efficient. Nervous and on my own, I landed in Moscow and was met by my contact, Dmitri. We took a taxi to Domodedovo Airport, a nerve-wracking experience in itself, as the driver reeked of vodka. We finally boarded a plane out to Chelyabinsk in Siberia, my destination for the next two weeks. I could write a book on that experience alone. I am English, and everyone was interested in me—and therefore wanted to ply me with vodka and talk about soccer. "It is very rude to refuse the vodka," Natalya, my gray-eyed and frankly gorgeous interpreter whispered in my ear while managing to avoid most of the drinks herself. To cut a long story short, I got the job done sort of, while adapting quickly to the Russian way of working about two hours per day. It was certainly an experience but very disorienting to begin with—and even more so when the vodka kicked in each day.
- In association with another consulting company, I ended up spending two weeks in various locations with a major brewing company in Venezuela. We were looked after every step of the way, picked up and dropped off by designated drivers, and housed in top hotels. And the work was interesting and engaging. All that didn't keep the Canadian consultant I traveled with from being paranoid the whole time, to the point of distraction, that we were going to be kidnapped. Needless to say, we were fine throughout, but I came to the conclusion that he should never have set foot outside North America.

Your reaction to the above two stories will tell you a lot about whether you want to pursue this type of work. If your reaction is that there's no way you want to go to Russia, period, and you feel the same as my colleague in

Venezuela, perhaps this sort of work isn't for you. Or perhaps it's location dependent, and you would be happy working in, say, Australia. On the other hand, if you relish the thought of being paid to go to some far-off places and having some out-of-the-ordinary experiences, maybe this sort of business is for you.

Like everything, international work has its pros and cons. It frequently pays better than work closer to home. On the other hand, it's much harder to keep projects nearer base going when you're on the other side of the world. Of course, being away from home for protracted periods also affects your family and your social life. And then there's all that hanging around at airports, losing your luggage, delayed flights, and the like, to deal with. Yet you get paid to travel to places you may not have visited otherwise, and you may be able to tack a vacation on at the end of your trip. Personally I've enjoyed most of the international travel I've done through my career: eighteen countries so far, with trips to Brazil and China lined up.

CHAPTER 7

Doing the Work

Not surprisingly, working occupies the majority of the time when you're a consultant, or at least it should. Funnily enough, it doesn't get the attention it deserves in books like this. How you interact with and communicate with your clients during projects is every bit as critical as the report you deliver, your final presentation, or the selling process that led you to the project. It's your opportunity to develop a great relationship that can serve you for years to come. There are some key things to be aware of as you work on a project, aside from the work itself.

What about the Client?

Consider this person we're calling the client. What's he doing for you, and what do you want from him?

- He's paying you for your services.
- He's talking about you to his boss, colleagues, and maybe friends at other organizations.
- He's the guy (usually) you'd like to sell another project to.
- He's the guy who can cause you a lot of problems and cost you a lot of time and money if he's unhappy.

So he's important. Okay, you knew that, didn't you? Well, then why do so many consultants lose sight of that fact as they work on projects?

Let's say you have a project with a deadline in six weeks. You know how to do it, you know what to do, and you can go away and do it. Do you know anything else?

- Why does he need the work completed?
- Why is there a deadline in six weeks?
- What depends on you hitting that deadline?
- Does he need anything during that six-week period—like an update?
- What can you do to make sure this is a very successful project—for him?

All of these questions are critical to your understanding of the project and your client. Knowing the answers can make the difference between your client perceiving you as just another consultant who did an okay job or someone he really feels good about and would hire again in a heartbeat.

Lots of consultants never consider any of this. They've got the job, and they go away and do it. They don't understand the background or rationale for the project. They don't communicate enough with the client. Just suppose your client's boss asks him how the project is going and if he's certain they're going to have the deliverables on time. If he hasn't heard from you in four weeks, he isn't going to be able to answer that question.

If you want more work out of your client; if you want some referrals or to use him as a reference; if you want to become his go-to consultant, you have to look beyond the basics. In fact, the extra time and effort to do this and to communicate regularly is minimal. So there's no excuse for not doing it, particularly when you consider the potential rewards it can bring. And at the end of the day, it's simply good, professional consulting, which should become second nature.

My Client Seems Irritated. What Have I Done?

Well, I don't know. What have you done? Or more likely, what haven't you done?

Of course it depends on the circumstances, but if you're detecting irritation, you may have a problem. Here are a few things that irritate a client—and yes, some of them were discovered firsthand, I'm ashamed to admit.

- Too little communication—the I-don't-even-know-if-you're-still-alive-syndrome.
- Badgering or pestering—"I've already told you I can't get that information until next week, so stop calling me."
- Invoices that don't comply with the client's company requirements.
- Expensing every little thing—"No, I don't expect to pay for your pens and paper. Get your own."
- Contacting your client's boss without permission. Going over your client's head is hardly ever a good idea.
- Being late—for meetings, calls, anything.
- Missing deadlines—it's never a good plan.
- Not telling your client about problems that will delay or jeopardize the project—you're ill for a week, your computer has a meltdown, and so on. Talk to your client about it as soon as you can.
- Getting frustrated with other people in the client's organization. Don't get mad because accounting wants copies of receipts for everything over a dollar; just comply.

We all make mistakes. Stuff happens. E-mail is misinterpreted. However, the better the relationship you have with your client, the less these things matter and the easier it is to get over them.

So your client seems irritated. Find out why—gently, calmly, firmly. It may be something else, nothing to do with you. If that's the case, ask him if there's anything you can do to help. Would it be better to defer the meeting, call, or whatever it is? Be sensitive to his needs, and don't judge; this is people management, not just client management.

Maybe it's because of you. Your client just received your latest invoice, and he's unhappy with it. Or the meeting was scheduled for ten, but you didn't arrive until 10:20. Whatever it is, find out. Then apologize. Then fix it and make sure you don't make that mistake again.

Finally, you can't get along with everyone. Sometimes there's simply a personality clash; you act professionally and don't let it show, but fundamentally you don't like this person. And in all probability, he doesn't like you. If that really is the case, the relationship is never going to prosper. So finish the project, do a good job, and accept that you won't be working for this person again.

What Happens If I Miss a Deadline?

If you miss a deadline you *may* have caused the following to happen:

- You've destroyed any trust and goodwill you've built up with your client.
- You've caused your client embarrassment, frustration, or anger, or all three.
- You've compromised your client's position in her organization.
- You've jeopardized the chances of your invoices being paid.
- You've destroyed the chance of any future work from either your client or her organization.
- You've damaged your reputation in the business circles frequented by your client.

Not good, not good. But on the other hand, you *may* have caused the following to happen:

- Nothing, no adverse effects, nothing at all.

It all depends on how you handled things in advance.

Apart from rare circumstances such as accidents or a sudden bout of amnesia, deadlines can't be missed, particularly the important ones. You realized that there was a good chance you wouldn't make the deadline some time ago. The big question is, what did you do about it at that time?

So why might you miss a deadline? It certainly isn't anything you plan. Here are a few possible reasons:

- Something weird happened: you were in a traffic accident, you were ill, you got stranded in Chicago due to a snowstorm.
- You underestimated the amount of work you had to do and couldn't get it all done in time.
- Someone who was supplying you with information or working on part of the project let you down.
- You needed some input from the client that wasn't forthcoming.

The solution to avoiding all the bad points listed at the start of this section is timely communication. Now, if something weird happens that is out of your control, you may not be able to communicate. However, I'd argue that this may be a result of poor planning on your part. Just because the deadline is November 1 doesn't mean you should plan to send it out at midnight on October 31 (after all that candy).

Consultants are famous for taking things to the wire, but it's not a good idea. And actually it's very bad for your blood pressure. It leaves no leeway; even if something minor happens, like your car breaks down, you could miss the deadline. If you have more time, you can probably still make it. Or you can talk to the client and warn him that you may not make it. That will probably not be a pleasant conversation, but it's much better than just failing to deliver.

Talk to the client. Remember, communication is critical—and never more so than when things are going out of control. If you realize a couple of weeks before that there's no way you can make the October 31 deadline, think about it logically. Why can't you make it? Is it a lack of information? Could you manage without that data? What *can* you provide by that date? If you can't complete by that date, when can you deliver by?

Talk to your client about it as soon as you can. Maybe the deadline isn't as critical after all. Maybe one part of the work is critical by that date but not the whole thing. Maybe that information you were waiting for isn't important after all. Until you start communicating, you simply won't know.

There's really no excuse, apart from dire emergency, for not delivering on time. It's unprofessional, and you open yourself up to the bad consequences mentioned above. It's *not* okay to be even a little late, unless you agreed on it with the client beforehand. If it was due on Monday and you delivered on Tuesday, you're late. Justifications like "It's only a day late" or "I nearly made the deadline" simply don't cut it.

How Do I Know If My Work Is Good Enough?

The first consulting company I joined had a phrase they used when undertaking work for a client. When you submitted your report for checking, prior to sending to the client, you'd be asked, "Did you go the extra mile?" Or worse, when you'd sweated over producing something on time and, you felt, to a high standard, you'd get the comment, "Hmm, it's okay, but I don't think you really went the extra mile." This honestly was a very depressing comment to hear.

Of course, what they meant was that we should exceed the clients' expectations; we should wow them to such an extent that they thought our company was the best thing since sliced bread and that they would be desperate to engage us again.

In fact, the projects were so tightly priced and our hourly fee rates (yes, those odious things) were so high, it was very difficult to do projects on time without working nights and weekends. And going the extra mile was almost impossible in many cases. Not surprisingly, the company never made any money and suffered hugely over the long haul.

When I look back on it twenty years later, I see that we lowly consultants were forced into doing way too much for what we charged. We did good work and gave good value and really didn't need to "go the extra mile." But this is with the benefit of hindsight. I remember struggling hugely at the time with what I needed to do to be good enough.

When you write a proposal or agree to a schedule of work with a client, as mentioned before, a lot of it is open-ended. So how far do you go? How deep do you dig? Well, if you know the background of the project, why your client needs the work done, and what he will need the results for, most of the time you know what you need to do. If you were in his shoes, what would you need?

Also, if you're keeping in regular communication with the client throughout the course of the project, part of that is letting him know in increasing detail what you'll be producing. So when you come up with the final report (or whatever it is), it won't come as a surprise to your client. And if he has some major problems with it, you have a paper trail on the basis of which you can start discussions. In my experience, most of the time a couple of minor tweaks is all that's needed.

Over time, you develop a feel for the standard that's expected by clients and also the level and depth of work that's realistic for the fees you're being paid. It's strange, but after a while you don't even have to think about it or be concerned over it. All you need is a year or two under your belt.

Finally, if your work is subpar in your client's eyes, believe me, you'll know pretty quickly. But really make an effort not to let it get to that stage. The key is to keep communicating throughout the course of the project. If you've just started out as a consultant, communication is even more critical. Don't be afraid to discuss the issue with your client if you're struggling to identify how deep you need to go. It's in her best interest for you to do a good job, and this is supposed to be a collaborative partnership.

I'd Like to Work with This Client Again, But How?

Here you are. You've reached the end of the project, done the final presentation, all has gone well, and you've been paid. Now what?

Let's say you enjoyed the work, liked the client, were happy with what you were paid, and would like to work for this client again. Here's what you know, or should know, if you've optimized your time along the way:

- a fair bit about the client personally
- something about the organization your client works for, the pressures she is under, the problems she experiences
- the number of other people in the client's organization, probably at a variety of levels and in a range of roles
- why the client commissioned the work you undertook and what part it played in the bigger picture
- where the client's organization is headed overall
- what references the client gave you (because you remembered to bring that up at an appropriate point, didn't you?)

There are probably a number of other things you know as well. So you know a lot. And you didn't know much of that when you started the project.

The easiest sale immediately follows the completion of your work. What would be of value to your client? Usually there's something. Or in the range of services you offer, is there someone else in the company who would benefit from something you can put forward? Or is there a problem your client has that you could help with? What would it be worth to your client if you could remove or at least alleviate that headache?

In short, use some imagination. I really enjoy this part of the work: thinking up how I can be of further value, taking my client out to lunch, and making a few suggestions.

Finally, exercise a little patience. Particularly if your client is with a large organization, the wheels grind very slowly. Your chances of finishing one project on Friday and starting the next the following Wednesday are low. It may take months for the next job to come around, even if you get tacit agreement to the work a few days later. The key to making it happen is to stay in touch and to tread that fine line between regular communication and becoming a nuisance. That can often mean communicating in a variety of ways, some of which aren't so direct, such as in a newsletter or a press release.

What If the Client Isn't Happy with What I've Done?

Have you ever felt like you're in a precarious position, balancing on a tightrope, and a small step in the wrong direction could end in disaster? This is exactly how I felt when I worked with Bob. A vice president in a large hotel chain, he was by far the most volatile client I've ever worked for. Large, aggressive, intimidating, and prone to violent fits of rage, he also was great company and very humorous when he was in a good mood. People are supposed to look like their dogs, and he owned two Rottweilers. Need I say more?

The first project I did for Bob was of a significant size (in terms of fees) and culminated in a report. I tried to communicate regularly during the project, but it was difficult; he was under a lot of pressure, answered e-mails rarely, and never answered his phone. So the job progressed with little input from him, and then I e-mailed him the draft report.

Then he communicated. I picked up my phone at nine one Monday morning and was greeted with a volley of expletives relating to me, my company, the work my team had done, and the standard of the report.

Well, to make a long story short, I went to see him, and as it turned out, he hadn't read the report properly, misinterpreted some of the conclusions, and was much happier (which wouldn't have been hard) when I ran through it with him. We made some modifications, added a bit more detail, clarified certain parts, and he was fine. The turning point in the meeting was when

I explained to him the problems I'd had communicating with him and that we'd had to make certain decisions without his input—the wrong decisions, as it turned out.

I worked with Bob for three more years until he retired, and he was one of my best clients. I hope this story illustrates a few useful points. If your client is unhappy, the first and most obvious question is "Why?"

If you've done a good job communicating with your client throughout your project, your client shouldn't be unhappy with the final report or whatever the end result is. However, it does still happen, even if you did everything right along the way. Possibly there has been a misinterpretation at some stage, or maybe the client expected a lot more detail than you provided. Sometimes the client has an idea of the outcome in mind, and what you've provided doesn't match up. In fact, when you're in the people business, as consultants are, there are many reasons a client may be unhappy. Having said that, in my experience, it doesn't happen often. But that doesn't make it any easier when it does.

Most of the time, if your client is unhappy, it's likely over fairly minor issues. My advice is to find out what they are and fix them as quickly as you can. Generally it isn't worth arguing or disagreeing unless it's a serious issue. The client is paying; if she asks for something minor to be added that you don't agree with, 95 percent of the time, it's quicker to just do what she wants.

If the client is seriously at odds with what you have produced, you have to discuss it and come to some agreement. For example, if the client is asking for something that's out of scope, you have every right to refuse to do it without additional fees (in a friendly, professional manner). If it's something you interpret as out of scope, but the client has the opposite view, this needs negotiation. It depends on how much work is involved to comply and whether or not you perceive ongoing value with this client. I've never experienced a situation that couldn't be resolved by discussion and negotiation with the client.

Finally, remember what a colleague of mine used to say: "Give the clients what they want, then sell them what they need." In other words, if the client wants something that doesn't make sense to you, provide what they want and then use that as a springboard to help them understand that *your* interpretation was what they *really* needed.

How Important Is the Final Presentation?

In short, the presentation is very important. It needs due consideration, preparation, and professional execution. But few consultants do a good job of it, mainly because they think they've already finished the project, and it's distracting them from their next piece of work.

The final presentation is a major opportunity for you for these reasons:

- You're showcasing your work and therefore enhancing your reputation.
- You're presenting personally and are thereby presenting and promoting yourself.
- You may be presenting to a range of people in the client organization, including perhaps staff at a more senior level than your main client contact.
- Your client contact's reputation may be enhanced if you do a good job and may diminish if you perform poorly.
- You get the chance to highlight potential for further work you could do.
- Because of the range of staff you may present to, you're likely to get a better understanding of the client organization.

I could go on, but I think you get the idea. There are a lot of potential benefits for you. Therefore, when you know you're committed to a final presentation, you need to do the following:

- Find out who will be attending, what their positions are, and any other details you can about them.

- Find out whether there are any sensitive issues you should avoid or key issues you should be sure to refer to.
- Check how long you should present for and what happens after your presentation. Is there time for questions, will there be lunch, et cetera?
- Find out where you will be presenting and what facilities will be available. Will the system be all set up? Should you use your own laptop?
- Check out what's at stake for your main client contact. Is there any way you can help him by mentioning something specific?
- Prepare your slides in advance, and run them by him first, so he can talk to you about anything he doesn't understand or may be unhappy with.
- Make sure you have all the details you need at your fingertips, and bring any backup information that you think may be required.
- Practice your presentation to make sure it flows and that you can fit it in the allotted time.

Overall, be as competent and professional as you can. This is your chance to make a good impression, enhance your reputation, and sell more work. Who doesn't want that?

Finally, if your client doesn't want a final presentation, try to persuade him otherwise. Sure, there are benefits for you, but there are also many positives for him if you do a good job.

Could I Have Done That Job Better?

Yes, you could, you always could, no matter how good you thought it was. This is why it's essential to take some time to review each project you undertake. Here are a few questions you might consider a few days after the end of the project, when the dust has settled a bit:

- Did I complete it in the hours I allocated?
- What went better than I expected?

- What went worse than I expected?
- What could I do to speed up my performance?
- What did I find difficult or problematic?
- What could I have done to make the project run more smoothly?
- On a one-to-ten scale, how much did I enjoy the work?
- On a one-to-ten scale, would I like to work with this client again?
- On a one-to-ten scale, what was the value to me from doing this work? (*Value* in this case takes into account everything: finances, enhancement of reputation, access to future work, and so on.)
- Overall, how do I rate my performance on a one-to-ten scale?

I suggest developing a questionnaire based on the above points and writing down your answers. It will be a useful reference for the future, because similar issues come up all the time. When you start a similar project a year down the line, it's very useful to be able to remind yourself what slowed you down on a previous project, what you should have done but didn't, and so on.

The other side of this equation is the client. No doubt you'll want to follow up with your client anyway, but it's worth getting her feedback. I suggest choosing an informal setting, such as over coffee or lunch. From the client's perspective, what was good and not so good? How could it have been better? Write all this down too.

The idea is that after every project you end up with a record you can refer to. On an ongoing basis, build in what you learned, and you'll become more effective. And what does that mean? Well, higher fee rates, more free time, more referrals, and a healthier forward pipeline of work. All that for an hour or two of analysis and soul searching has always seemed to be a good deal to me.

CHAPTER 8

Show Me the Money!

It's nice to get paid, isn't it? After all, when all is said and done, the whole idea was to make a living out of this consulting thing. But believe it or not, some people shy away from the money side of their business in a belief that it will look after itself or something. Give it the attention it deserves.

Why Is Cash Flow So Important?

Cash is king. Any financial director of any business will tell you that. And from your consulting business to Google to General Electric, the story is the same. Businesses more often fail from lack of cash than from a lack of orders or a lack of work. If you've ever run a small business, this message came over loud and clear to you. But if you're just starting out, it may not be so obvious. Let's paint a picture.

Say you need $8,000 per month to run your business, pay the mortgage, feed the kids, and so on. Therefore you need to invoice enough to net that amount every month to keep your finances on an even keel. If only things in consulting were so easy. Here are a few reasons things may go wrong:

- Your work is variable; some months you invoice $15,000, others $5,000 or less.

- Clients pay at different rates and times: some on completion, some one month after completion, some with partial payments during the course of the project.
- Sometimes sales roll in the door; other times the door seems to be slammed shut.
- Project starts get delayed, and the work you were expecting to do in September is pushed back to January.
- Projects in progress get delayed, and you can't invoice for another couple of months
- Projects get canceled. (Aargh!)
- Clients "lose" your invoices or "forget" to pay you.
- You're ill and can't work for a couple of weeks.

And things looked so easy when you started. So in our little scenario, you may have just experienced three months in a row with very little coming in. But the kids still need feeding, the mortgage still needs paying, and your borrowing limit is getting ever closer. It doesn't matter that there's $72,000 invoiced and owed to you; the fact is that you don't have the cash and you need it *now*. All of a sudden, your stress levels are hitting the roof, you can't sleep, and you're wondering how you ever got yourself into such a mess.

Okay, I'm painting a black picture, but those scenarios happen all too often—and I've been there. I know what it's like. Fortunately there are lots of actions you can take to prevent this from happening to you, as explained in the following sections of this chapter. Believe me, waking up at three in the morning stressing about your lack of cash flow is no fun at all.

Yes, cash is king; it really is.

How Do I Invoice My Clients for Fees and Expenses?

An invoice is simply a means to an end. All an invoice does is tell the client what you think you're owed. The overriding objective, of course, is to enable you to be paid as soon as possible. So it's essential that your invoice is

- clear and easy to understand;
- descriptive as far as it needs to be in relation to the project you're doing;
- includes any necessary references, such as a purchase order number;
- complies exactly with your client's purchasing department requirements; and
- includes appropriate taxes.

Okay so far? Easy. But there's much more to the art of invoicing. And while invoicing may seem to be a fairly simple process, it can cause you great problems with your clients if you get it wrong. Also, remember that the main object is for you to get paid as quickly and as efficiently as possible. So here are a few things to consider.

When do you invoice?

Most consultants invoice at the end of each month; that's what I've done most of the time in my consulting career. If everything goes according to plan, you should get paid approximately one month after your invoice is received. Therefore, if you start a project on September 1 and invoice on September 30, all being well, you'll be paid around October 31. In other words, you've completed two months of work before you see any cash at all. With cash being king and all that, that's less than ideal.

One way to improve cash flow is to invoice up front. So if the project is three months long, invoice one third on receiving the go-ahead, one third after month one, and the remainder after month two.

Usually you state your invoicing schedule within your proposal, and if it's a new client, it should have been discussed at a prior meeting. In my experience, most private clients are happy to pay reasonable upfront invoices. However, generally public clients, such as governments, utilities, and municipalities, are not. In these cases, unless you can negotiate something specifically, you will take the cash-flow hit.

How much do you invoice?

Invoice as much as you think is reasonable. One way is to divide the job up time-wise, so a five-month job is invoiced at a rate of 20 percent per month. This is fine except when the work on a project is weighted toward the front end. In that case, there's nothing wrong with, for example, the first two invoices each for 35 percent of the total and the remaining three at 10 percent.

What about expenses?

In my experience, more problems are caused with invoicing expenses than anything else. The neatest way is to avoid expenses altogether by simply agreeing on a total price for your services, including fees and expenses. One company I know quotes its fees and adds 8 percent to cover expenses, which is okay except when your client knows that expenses will be a very small component of total job costs.

If you're on a project where you're required to break down expenses, make it clear and simple, and please, please, err on the side of omitting anything you think may cause a problem. In other words, if you bought a new pen or legal pad, don't charge those costs. If you had seven cups of coffee that day, charge two at most, but preferably none. You may laugh at these examples, but I've seen both and many more besides. Think of the client reactions: "I'm paying you $200 an hour, and you can't pay for your own paper?" or "Why should I fund your caffeine addiction?"

On a final note, if you have any concern about your invoice prior to sending it, notify your client and discuss it, if need be. It's far quicker and will be perceived as more professional to preempt an invoice problem than to send it and deal with the fallout.

What About Taxes?

Yes, you have to pay them. Personal tax, business tax, sales tax—there's no escaping any of it, although there are numerous strategies to minimize your payments. However, unless you happen to be a tax consultant, this isn't your field. Find someone who can look after all of this for you. After all, you probably don't service your own car or fix your own plumbing. (Or do you?) Some things are best left to those who know that field. And it's cost-effective because it leaves you time to earn money at something you're good at.

That said, in terms of getting the money into the business, you need to make sure you include the appropriate taxes on your invoices. Most commonly, this involves sales tax in some form or another, depending on where you live and where your client is. My business is based in British Columbia, Canada, and any fees I invoice in Canada are subject to 5 percent General Sales Tax (GST). When I'm paid, I retain that tax on behalf of the government and submit payments to them quarterly, net any GST I have incurred through, for example, buying a new laptop. Fees for work that I do overseas don't require GST to be added.

As previously stated, it depends on where you live and who you work for. Just make sure you find out what's required in your area, and get it right. There's nothing like an ongoing tax issue to suck up all your time and leave you wondering why you didn't check on it months before.

What Are Terms and Conditions, and Do I Need My Own?

Have you ever read the "Terms and Conditions" on anything? When we download the latest software update, we check the "I agree to the terms and conditions" box first. But do we read the three tightly scripted pages of legalese and scrutinize every word before we agree? If you do, I suggest you're in the minority—the tiny, tiny minority. Really the only people who read this stuff generally are lawyers. The rest of us don't have the time, don't care, don't understand it anyway, and couldn't stay awake long enough to read it if we tried.

So do you need a page or two of incomprehensible legalese at the end of your proposal? It depends on who you ask. If you ask me, I'd say no.

Now that anyone in the legal profession or a large consulting company has written me off as reckless at best or words unprintable at worst, let me expand a little. Terms and conditions are as described: the terms and conditions under which you perform the work. So aren't you sorting this out anyway in your discussions leading up to the proposal and in the proposal itself? If you want to add a document that lays out your insurance limits, your invoice payment requirements, your policies on confidentiality, your limitation of liability, and so on, fine. However, in my experience, it can be a major source of contention, particularly if you're dealing with a big company that has lawyers specifically employed to analyze and argue these sorts of issues. That is time, money, and delay, and you're probably going to concede the points eventually anyway.

For the great majority of consulting projects, there's no need for a catch-all terms and conditions section in your proposal. If there are specific issues relating to risk to your company for a particular project, address those up front in your proposal. You'll always be insured for any unforeseen issue you could get blamed for. (Won't you?)

I guess it really comes down to how much this sort of stuff concerns you. If you're lying awake at night worried that you should have included risk-covering statements in your latest proposal, you need to get terms and conditions drafted. Hire a lawyer, get it done, and go back to sleep. Personally I can nod off without them. If I have trouble sleeping, I start reading some.

How Important Is It to Follow Up on My Unpaid Invoices?

Well, isn't it obvious? It's very important. It's more important than the project you're working on, the proposal due next week and, the client meeting you're off to this afternoon. Remember, cash is king. So making sure people who owe you pay up is the most important thing you can do.

This is obvious to me and to lots of people in consulting—or any business, for that matter. But strangely it's not important to everyone. The first consulting company I worked in was terrible about this. They were actually appalling in all aspects of collecting the money. I remember one project we completed for a large brewing company. It was a lot of work in a short space of time, and the organization was difficult to deal with and very demanding. Somehow we got through the final presentation and all heaved a sigh of relief.

I found out later that the project manager forgot to invoice until three months later, and then we didn't get paid for another five months after that. I'd like to say that was a one-off, but it was almost normal. It was as though the invoicing and cash collection were just too mundane to deal with. As soon as the company started having cash-flow problems, the situation tightened up. (Surprise, surprise.) It should never have reached that point in the first place.

Consider the unpaid invoice situation. You've committed time and expertise, and you paid out some expenses. You've fulfilled your side of what is supposed to be a partnership. You have every right to expect to be paid within a reasonable amount of time. (In most cases, I expect to be paid within a month.) So if it hasn't happened, make it a priority to follow up.

When you follow up, speak to your client contact, not to the accounts department. It's the client who you have a relationship with, and it should be up to her to ensure that you get your money. And don't be shy about following up time and time again, if that check still hasn't arrived. Let's face it; if the relationship has regressed to them getting you to work for free, that isn't a relationship you will be keen to continue.

What Should I Do If Someone Delays Payment?

I don't know of anyone in the consulting business—or in any business—who this hasn't happened to: The invoice is due, you're waiting for the money to drop into your account or a check to arrive in the mail. And you wait and you wait. As described in the previous section, you follow up with the client. It's a business priority, remember?

Typically you'll face one of four scenarios:

- Administrative problems. The company has "lost" your invoice or thought they'd already paid you or used the wrong payment code or … In this case, they want to pay you, but, hey, mistakes happen. Or they're just inept. Whatever reasons you assign and however frustrated you are, it's usually easily rectified.
- They're unhappy with the invoice and didn't bother to tell you. You miscoded it, didn't put it in the right form, got the project reference wrong, or something else. Simply apologize, submit a correct version, and mark your cash-flow problems down as "Hey, mistakes happen" or your own ineptness.
- They're unhappy with the invoice and didn't bother telling you because they don't think they owe you that much, or they refuse to pay for the seven cups of coffee you charged to the project last Tuesday or … Talk to the client. Go and see them if necessary. You have to get to the bottom of this one. In my experience, as long as you're prepared to be reasonable, a compromise can usually be reached.
- They keep saying they've passed the invoice for payment and it's in the payment process, but the cash never appears. This is the scenario where alarm bells should start ringing for you. They appear to be stringing you along, and you're probably doing additional work for them as time rolls by, possibly putting you into a bigger loss situation. In this situation, stop work on the project and set that down formally in an e-mail to your client. State also that project deadlines agreed in the proposal will now no longer be met. Also ask for a meeting with your client.

I experienced this last scenario once and found out the company was suffering cash-flow problems. If you have the feeling that this might be the case, when you go into the next project, demand your fees up front.

What Should I Do If Someone Refuses to Pay?

Hopefully you face this situation very rarely, if ever. Delaying a payment is one thing; flat-out refusing to pay is another. If your client is uttering those words, things have gone badly wrong and should never have reached that stage.

Once this happened to me. I set up and signed a contract with a medium-sized consulting company. The CEO of the company also signed it. Basically it consisted of a finder's fee percentage for work I brought to the company plus a deal on projects that I worked on with the company. All was fine until I found them a $50,000 project and claimed my finder's fee. At that point, the CEO refused to pay, saying that he should never have agreed to the fee. I pointed to our agreement, and he still refused. And so on and so on. Eight months later, I got the money out of him after pursuing legal action. I've never worked with him or his company since, and I never did find out what the problem was.

So if you're unlucky, this can happen.

If a client just simply refuses to pay and won't compromise, listen to reason, or respond to your multiple payment demands, you have two (unpleasant) options:

1. Write it off as bad debt. Of course, this depends on how much it is and what you think your chances are of getting paid eventually. I know this seems like giving in, but think about the time, effort, and stress that you will incur trying to get that invoice paid. Would you be better off conducting or pursuing work with someone you can work with?
2. Take legal action, starting with a lawyer's letter and escalating from there, if needed. If you choose this option, weight the associated costs, the likelihood of a favorable settlement, and the stress and anxiety involved.

Finally, if a client chooses not to pay you, never ever work with them again. Not even if you eventually get your money.

Should I Increase My Rates from Time to Time?

George is a subcontractor who works for me from time to time. He's competent, honest, trustworthy, personable, fun to work with—and in seven years he still charges his time to me (and everyone else) at the same hourly rate. I'd pay him more—and even foolishly mentioned this to him once—but he still keeps the same rates.

Should George increase his rates? I think so. Even if you estimate inflation at only 2 percent per year, over seven years that compounds to 15 percent. So George is working for 15 percent less than he was seven years ago. Also he is seven years older, wiser, and more experienced. Certainly he should be charging more.

So that's George. How about you? Well, as mentioned before, you should be charging based on the value you're delivering to the client, not the number of hours you work. So quoting a fee rate is probably not appropriate. However, as mentioned before, you should be working out what your hourly earnings are, and that value should be increasing over time. If it's flat lining or going down, there's something you have to fix. Like George, you're now accepting less for your time and skills than you were before.

If you're in the unenviable position of having to quote a fee rate, my advice is to increase it annually at a rate you feel is fair. This allows you to take into account inflation and your increasing expertise. It's much easier for a client to accept an annual fee rate increase than a sudden, large increase after five years.

If George hits me with a seven-year increase ... I'll happily pay him.

How Do I Know If I'm Making Money?

Have you ever watched *Dragons' Den* or *Shark Tank*? In these TV programs, entrepreneurs pitch their ideas and try to entice the "dragons" or "sharks" to invest in their ideas. The ideas range from boneheaded to brilliant, but it always amazes me how many of the contestants bomb on what should be simple questions, like "What were your sales last year?" and "What is your profit margin?"

If you can't answer questions like that about your own business, no one will invest in you. And when you're consulting, it's the same. You should know how much money you're making.

Consulting really is a very simple business, particularly if your business is you. All you're doing is selling your time and expertise for money. So if you quote $20,000 for a project, thinking that it will take one hundred hours, but it actually takes three hundred, your hourly rate is less than $67 per hour. You're still making money, but not enough. And I suspect it's nowhere near what you planned to make when you decided to go into consulting (see chapter 2).

So the subtitle question above really should be "How Do I Know How Much Money I'm Making?" And it's easy, really easy, to work this out. All you need to do is log the hours you spend on each project and the hours you spend on non-fee-earning work, like marketing, taking your clients to a game, buying them drinks until they fall over, and so on. And then do some arithmetic. You spent 100 hours on that project and earned $40,000. Congratulations! You earned $400 an hour. But if that was the only project you did all year and you put in 1,900 hours non-fee-earning time, then you took 2,000 hours to earn $40,000, which works out at $20 per hour. But you bought all those game tickets and drinks, so it wasn't even that good.

Okay, maybe you're rolling your eyes now. So am I. But just keep some records; that's all you need to do.

CHAPTER 9

Pitfalls and Problems

You didn't expect any problems, did you? Well, it wouldn't be real life without a few problems, and the consulting business you're embarking on or are already involved in is no exception. In a way, the problems make it even more interesting, although they may seem like interest you could do without. The good news is that 99.9 percent of them can be overcome and, if you can recognize them early, sorting them out is much easier. I've experienced all the issues outlined in the next few sections, and if I'd had better advice early on, I'd have been much happier. If only I'd found a book like this one.

What If the Work Takes Longer Than I Thought?

A couple of chapters ago, we dealt with what happens if you miss a deadline. One obvious reason is that the work took longer than you thought. Let's deal with the root causes of the work taking so long.

First, take some solace in the fact that every consultant, even the most experienced ones, occasionally falls into this position. It will happen to you from time to time, and there are a number of ways you can deal with it:

- Overrun the deadline. This isn't recommended, as discussed earlier.

- Put in the extra hours, work day and night, and simply suck it up. At least the client will happy. But I bet you won't.
- Identify what particular parts of the work are taking so long and find ways to shortcut them or speed them up. This often works very well.
- Talk to the client and explain the situation. Remember, you're supposed to be in partnership with your client, so you don't need to suffer in silence.
- Explain to your client that you need more fees to complete the project. This is never an easy conversation. You need to have a good case as to why you deserve more fees for a project that hasn't changed since you proposed it.

As always, there are a number of potential approaches, and which you choose depends on the reasons the job is taking longer and how soon you identify that this is an issue.

What Is Scope Creep?

No, it has nothing to do with stalking or creeping, or being a creep. It's not even a criminal activity. But it's a criminal waste of time for consultants.

So what is it? It's the not-so-gentle art some clients have of persuading you to do more than they're actually paying you for. Let me give you a few examples.

- "We're bringing all our sales guys together for a meeting next week. Could you come along and give them a quick presentation on what you're doing?"
- "I know we asked you just to focus on helping our IT section, but HR could benefit from a quick refresher on the system. It will only take a couple of hours."
- "Yes, but we restructured that part of the company since you started the work, so I expect you to cover all the functions in that section, not just what was there two months ago."

Get the picture? Unfortunately this happens a lot and can put you in a difficult situation. You want the client to be happy and satisfied with the work you do. Equally, it would be nice to make some money on the project. And you'd like another project from this client after this one.

Think about it in a different situation, and it looks ridiculous: Try demanding a second dessert for free in a restaurant. Or ask an interior decorator to paint the outside while he's there—for no extra cash.

Yet scope creep doesn't always come from the client. I've been in meetings with other consultants who have initiated their own scope creep with ill-placed comments like these:

- "We can look at that as well, if you'd like."
- "I can do that for you as part of this project."
- "It's no problem to run a couple of extra training sessions within the contract."

And How Do I Avoid It?

If you're initiating the scope creep, I think you know the answer to this question. If the client initiates, this is a $64,000 question. (Why $64,000? I've always wondered.) Like most issues in consulting, you deal with it on a case-by-case basis by being firm and professional and talking it through with your client.

Of course, it depends on how much extra the client is asking for, how much you value the client, whether it's actually scope creep or just a different interpretation of the contract, and so on. It will also depend on how the job has progressed so far. If things went far easier than you anticipated, you'll probably be more amenable to doing a little bit extra than if the opposite happened.

Fundamentally you shouldn't allow any scope creep. It's extra work you're not being paid for. In practice, you'll probably accept a little bit now and again as a gesture of goodwill. You should never—and I repeat never—accept extra work without letting the client know it's outside the specifications. Statements like "This is actually outside the contract, but I'm happy to cover it in in this instance" generally serve the purpose.

The difficulty doesn't come so much with little things that you're prepared to cover at no extra cost. It comes when the client asks for something that's really going to cause you problems in terms of additional time and effort. In this case, you have to be firm and say that you can't do that within the scope of the project. You can say you'd be happy (if you are) to provide a quotation for the extra work. Or perhaps you're prepared to cover a small part of the additional work at no extra cost.

If the client gets upset, that's an unpleasant situation to be in, but you have to stick to your guns. This is supposed to be a professional partnership, so you have a right to make some profit on the project. If the client won't budge, you simply have to refuse to do the additional work and accept that you're probably not going to work for him again. But if your client acts like that, you probably don't want to work with him again anyway.

The vast majority of clients are reasonable, and I've never had a serious case of scope creep that hasn't been resolved amicably, even when I've said no. After all, you aren't saying no just to be difficult; you're saying no because it's not reasonable to be expected to do a significant amount of extra work for nothing. Just stand your ground, be firm, and if you feel it's appropriate, throw in the decorating or restaurant analogy. Sometimes it just adds that extra bit of perspective.

They Keep Calling Me for Free Advice

In a way, this is scope creep, except that you don't even have a scope yet! And it can be more insidious and more time consuming. The phrase that seems to come up most frequently is "pick your brain." As soon as I hear those three words, the alarm bells start ringing for me. Typically the phone call or e-mail goes like this: "A situation arose the other day, and I wonder if you might be able to help us. If we could meet for coffee one day next week and I could just pick your brain for a few minutes ..."

What happens next? It depends on who it is, whether you know her, whether she has been referred by someone who knows you, and so on. In any case, the implication is that you might get a project out of the meeting, so probably you go along. The trouble is that you don't know yet if there *will* be a new project.

In my experience, there's often no chance of new work; it's literally what the caller said: she wants your expertise for free. But a commitment to coffee can be quite sizable on your part. By the time you've deferred other work you have planned, taken the time to get there, given free consulting for an hour, and travelled back to your office, it's at least a couple of hours out of your day.

So what should you do? Well, you have to decide when enough is enough, and this means being firm with a potential client. Clearly express to her that you're very happy to help, but that you can't commit your time for free. Suggest that perhaps she would like to set up a call off contract with you for a few hours that she can draw on as issues arise. Or ask if you can submit a proposal to her to help with the work you would be talking about over coffee.

You have to move her away from considering you to be a free resource. If that means being very forthright to someone who just won't get the message, so be it. You're a valuable resource; otherwise she wouldn't want your help. It's only fair that she pays for it.

At least in that coffee scenario, there may be a possibility of some return on your time and knowledge commitment. But there's also the caller who says something like this: "I'm thinking about getting into the accounting / IT / sustainability (or whatever) field, and I was wondering if you'd have time for a coffee in the next week or two so I can pick your brain."

In this case, there is practically zero chance that you'll get any work from this encounter. That isn't to say you should never go help people; just be aware that you're in the pro-bono realm in this situation.

A friend of mine is a highly accomplished consultant who frequently earns $500 per hour or more. He got so disillusioned with the requests for "pick your brain" coffee meetings that he developed this response: "I typically earn $500 per hour. Pay me $500, and I'll happily come and have coffee with you. If it results in a contract for me, I'll deduct the $500 from the contract fees."

He tells me that works pretty well. Can't say I'm surprised.

What If the Client Is Never Satisfied?

Typically the conversation goes something like this:

"I'm not very happy with the level of detail in section X of your report. Could you just strengthen it a bit?"

"Thanks for that, but now that I think about it, we really need a section in there on Y."

"Okay, nearly there I think, but I'm not very happy with the flow of the document."

And so on, down to "I think we could have gotten away with a comma instead of a semicolon in the first sentence on page 21." By this time, any hair you had left has gone gray or been torn out, and your thoughts have turned to murder. Okay, I'm exaggerating a bit, but you get the picture. Yes, there are clients like that. Fortunately they're usually limited by time constraints on the overall project—but unfortunately not always. So what do you do apart from scream?

Well, as usual, this comes down to communication—and, in this case, firm communication. Everyone accepts some changes at the client's request, but there has to be a limit. When the limit is crossed, every e-mail, call, meeting, and revision is eating into your profit until there is none left. Eventually you simply have to refuse.

I recommend setting out the case clearly, something like: "We have now revised the document three times, and I trust that we've covered all the points you raised. I attach the final version. Please note that we cannot make any further revisions without an amendment to our fees."

If that causes problems, so be it. You simply can't go on making changes forever; you're running a business and are supposed to be working in partnership with your client.

Finally, when it's all over, and your hair is growing back, take time to meet with your client. In my experience, it's worth both of you giving the other feedback. He may not have realized the extent of the problems you suffered. Equally, there may have been something that you didn't appreciate or understand or something you did that caused the client problems. If you can clear the air, you may get to a point where you feel happy taking on another project with this client. Or you may not.

What Should I Do If I "Fall Off a Cliff'?

No matter what you read, who you listen to, what actions you take, or how skilled you are, the chances are you or your company will fall off a cliff. Of course it shouldn't—we all know that. It's like saying you shouldn't get into debt or you shouldn't have had that seventh jager bomb. Stuff happens for whatever reason, and before you know it, you've committed the ultimate consulting sin of falling off a cliff.

Falling off a cliff doesn't have an official definition, I don't think. As discussed before, it means finishing all the paid work you had and then having nothing. It's an easier trap to fall into if your consulting company is small rather than large—and particularly if small means just you.

So a typical scenario looks like this: You're really busy with that big project you sold—you know, the ones with the tight deadlines. Suddenly you find it takes up all your time, and you're not devoting any effort to getting more work in the door. So surprise, surprise, the big project finishes, and you have no more work and no prospects. Or perhaps you did have something lined up, but that client has delayed the start for three months—or canceled it.

You were on the green grass up top, and now you're on the beach, looking up, and the tide is coming in. Well, join the club. Most of us have been there.

The first thing to do is not panic or beat yourself up mentally. Take solace in the fact that most of us have been there. It's not the end of the world; it's just that *temporarily* you don't have any work. If you have just come off a very busy period of work, presumably the fees from that will keep the tide back for a while. So this may be a blessing in disguise. For once you have time to think about your business, plan, strategy—that sort of stuff.

The second thing to do is try to get some more work in the door. Note the emphasis on the word *temporarily* in the paragraph above. Just because you have a blip in your workload doesn't mean that's how things will remain. You got projects before; you'll get them again. And with the extra time you now have, you can go about that in a structured, logical way, which will increase your likelihood of success. There's a whole chapter on getting work (chapter 6), so go back and take a look if you need a couple of ideas.

Finally, don't throw away your principles or values. Don't accept a contract with a lower value than you would normally, simply because you have no work at this point. In my experience, that will only hurt you in the long-run by diminishing your value. You know what you're worth, and this cliff in front of you doesn't change that.

Okay, I'll stop preaching.

I Really Don't Like This Person

We all know what's supposed to happen. The consulting arrangement is a partnership, and as with all partnerships, we get along great. I enjoy meeting with Diane. She's a great client—fun, upbeat, positive, understanding, professional. In fact, working with her isn't like work at all. That's how it should be, right?

Yes, of course. But there'd never be any divorces if we all got along. So there will be clients you don't get along with. The question is what, if anything, you do about it.

Joe was a client I'd describe as a low reactor. He didn't say much and seemed uncomfortable in any sort of social situation, even if we were just having coffee together and talking about the project. He always seemed irritable and offhand, and I didn't enjoy working with him.

As the project progressed, he became grumpier. I asked him a few times if he was unhappy with the project, but he would never tell me. Toward the end of the work, with him acting worse and worse toward me, I decided to sort this out. At a meeting in his office, I told him I had been experiencing negativity from him throughout, which I didn't feel I deserved. I said that I had asked him on several occasions whether there was something at fault with my performance on the project and had never been told there was. Hence, I didn't know what the problem was, but I wanted to be treated with more civility from that point on.

There was silence, and for a minute I thought he was going to explode. Then it all came out. He had wanted to carry out this work personally, but his boss had insisted he contract it out and had implied that he wasn't capable of doing the work adequately. Hence his hostile attitude toward me, which he apologized for.

We got on better from that point on, and he did go out of his way to be pleasant to me. Nevertheless, after finishing that project, I decided I did not want to work with him again.

CHAPTER 10

Successful Strategies

A consulting practice is always changing as you take on different clients and different work, as you gain experience, as you move into different markets, and so on. And because it keeps changing, it's easy to lose sight of the big picture. Hence, it's essential to develop a few strategies and techniques to keep you on track and make life easier for yourself.

Should I Allocate Time to Review?

Probably you're thinking that the answer is obvious: of course you should. And you're right. But the reason for this section is that so many consultants either fail to do it ever or do it in a way that isn't objective and is of little worth.

In theory, you need to set aside a significant chunk of time—a couple of days at least. Then you carry out an objective review, looking at all the metrics of your business and answering questions like these:

- Has my hourly rate increased?
- Am I happy with the time and effort I put in?
- Where is my work coming from, and what can I do to increase the workflow and sales success?
- What are my plans for the coming year, and am I going to try to expand my skills and services?

After all this soul searching and brain strain, you come up with a strategic plan for the next twelve months and head off to even greater success.

Well, that's the plan, but how many of us actually do it? You may make some plans, but are you finding time to do that blue-sky thinking on how to make your business and your life better? Even if you intend to, can you actually do it? It's hard to be objective, particularly when you're trying to do this stuff on your own. It's all too easy to check your e-mails and carry on working on existing projects, using that time you set aside for reviewing.

There are no magic bullets here. If you're 100 percent happy with how your consulting business is rolling along, you don't need to review. However, if like most of us, you feel some improvements should be made, you owe it to yourself to try to get your head around things.

Bottom line, a review is worth doing, and it's worth doing properly. So set the time aside, and plan what you're going to do and how you're going to do it. Also plan where you're going to do it; sitting in your home office with its distractions may not be the best place. Perhaps you need to get out somewhere. Perhaps you need to exercise and do your thinking after that— or during it maybe. At the end of the day, it's whatever works for you.

Just please don't let it slip by. You can't improve your business unless you take the time to consider the issues properly.

What Is the Ideal Workload?

The ideal workload is the workload that works for you, not someone else. Maybe you started your business with a plan to take six weeks of vacation a year and work standard office hours. If last year you took two weeks of vacation and spent half of that on your laptop, I suggest the original plan has stretched a bit. Now, that may be fine, as long as you're happy with it, and it isn't causing major problems in other areas, such as in your family. If it isn't working out for you, and what you really wanted was plan A, you need to reassess.

The situation described above is typical of many small or individual consulting companies. The hours stretch, other commitments get lost (particularly family), vacations get shortened or disappear altogether. Before you know it, you're working way too hard, and you and those around you are suffering. If this is the case, you need to get back on track. You really do.

How Can I Improve My Sales Success Rate?

If you haven't done it already, you need to do some analysis. Look back at your projects over the last couple of years and recall how you got them. Did you win them in open RFPs? Were they the result of people you met at certain types of events? How many clients are new? What size of project are you typically selling? Which were your best projects? Are there any patterns you can see?

Then do an analysis of your unsuccessful proposals. Do you know why they were unsuccessful? What is the ratio of proposals to sales? What is the dollar ratio of proposals to sales? Do you know how long you spent on proposals? Again, are any patterns emerging?

Some indicators may drop out of this analysis. Typical results include the following:

- A lot of time is spent responding to RFPs unsuccessfully.
- Most of your sales are coming from one major client or one sector.
- A lot of proposals are what you might regard as long shots.
- Most of the projects sold are low in value.

Okay, now let's turn this around. Who is your ideal client or which is your ideal sector? How are you targeting that sector? Where do you need to be to meet more people in that sector? How are your sales and marketing activities geared to your ideal clients and sectors?

Then there's research. Do you know what the key issues are in your target sector? Do you understand the problems your ideal clients are struggling with? Can you think of any services you can offer that may help them? And if you can identify some issues, can you come up with some marketing activities that would help get your name out there?

There are no silver bullets in this area, in my experience. But there are a couple of things you can do to radically improve your chances:

- There is no substitute for face-to-face contact, so get out to the appropriate networking events where your ideal clients are, so you can get yourself better known within that sector.
- Speaking at an event that your ideal clients may attend is a gold-plated opportunity to get more work. Find an appropriate event, even a small one, that you can present at. This can have a huge impact.

Obviously, increased sales success has a direct impact on the viability of your business. If you're struggling, applying the correct strategies in this area will turn your business around. (And that's going to be the subject of my next book.)

How Do I Get a Steady Monthly Income?

Wouldn't it be boring to have a regular amount of cash dropping into your bank account every month? A bit like that dull job you used to have, maybe? Well yes, but it's nice to know that a healthy minimum amount is coming in each month. So how do you get that?

Well, I've written extensively in this book about the feast-or-famine, falling-off-a-cliff scenario. This is the exact opposite. Ideally what you need is one or more of the following:

- A large multiyear project for which you're contracted to bill a certain amount each month. I had a three-year project with a large utility that brought in $10,000 every month, minimum.
- A number of smaller long-term projects that sum up to the same.

- A few call-off contracts, which are good work if you can get them; you charge a monthly sum on an ongoing basis to be available for advice.
- Lots of repeat work, so you don't need many new clients. You know that a large percentage of your fees will roll in from existing clients year after year.

In practice, getting a steady basic income is hard when you start up. However, after you're better established, it's much easier; you have a long track record and repeat business, you can charge more, and so on. All being well, you'll get to a steadily growing monthly income, which most people agree is way better than a steady one.

Do I Contract Work Out or Do It All Myself?

A decision to contract out should be based on a number of factors. When I think back on work that I've contracted out, my reasons have been as follows:

- It's more economical for me to concentrate on other work and pay someone else to do the work I've decided to contract.
- I simply don't have time to do the work, so I pay someone to help me.
- I don't have the skill set for that part of the work, so I pay someone who does.
- I have little interest in that work, so I get someone else to do it and take a cut.

There are a few issues associated with using subcontractors. For a start, you have to trust them both from a business and from a general capability viewpoint. Then there's the question of whether you'll allow them to interact with your client or not. And of course you have to decide how much to pay them, the terms of the deal you set up, and so on. All this varies hugely from project to project.

I often work on a two-thirds / one-third split. This means that if I get a $15,000 project that a subcontractor is going to handle for me, I pay her $10,000. This leaves me $5,000 to add to my bank account while I laze around the pool.

But I still have responsibility for the project; I still have to make sure the final product is to an acceptable standard; I still have to deal with the client from time to time; I still have to be there at the final presentation; I always have to consider that it's my company's reputation resting on this work, and so on. All these issues can severely limit your time in the sun. Nevertheless, if your subcontractor is good, it's still a good deal.

So, in theory, you can subcontract everything and live at the pool, except for those few points I mentioned above. And you do need to keep the work coming in. If you want to earn $200,000 per year, that means you need to sell $600,000 if you keep the same payment ratio going. That isn't a problem—maybe—but it's certainly something to think about.

CHAPTER 11

Taking Your Business to the Next Level

If you've been in business for a while, you may feel you've reached a point where you can effect a substantial change. It may not be a dramatic event, such as acquiring another company; it may be a personal decision to do something differently or to take more vacation. Whatever it is, it needs to be addressed, giving you some things to think about.

What Do You Want?

One of the great things about having your own business is the ability to make choices. It's your business, and no one is going to tell you that you can't do that or that it doesn't fit in with overall company strategy. The decision is yours, and that applies to any business, not just consulting.

However, a consulting business is a lot more flexible than, say, an ice cream manufacturer or a welding shop. So I believe it's a mistake to put a box around your business and restrict yourself to being an IT consultant, for example. There's nothing wrong with that, of course. But we all like to dream, and as a consultant, you probably have more opportunity than most to make it a reality.

So what do you want? Jane is a technical consultant supplying services to a range of international companies. She works hard, puts in a lot of hours, and travels the world. As a result, it's been tough for her to switch off and take a break. When I asked her a few years ago if she was satisfied with her work-life balance, she nodded happily. "Adrian, I love being paid to go to interesting places and do what I do," she said.

Five years later, it was a different story. The traveling and the technical consulting had become stale, and she was easing herself out of that work. Her plan was to develop skills as a mentor to younger staff in certain industry sectors, and she was well on her way to achieving that goal.

The point of Jane's story is that we all change and need different things out of our work as well as the rest of our lives. Jane made a decision about what she wanted to do and then made the necessary changes to allow her to follow that path. She could have done what so many people do: stay with work that is no longer fulfilling. For consultants, change is part of the overall package, but I know a number of consultants who've become stuck in a rut of their own making.

We all know when we aren't happy, and we all know when we're bored or unfulfilled. I think the secret is to preempt these undesirable states of mind as much as you can by doing some self-analysis. Find a time when you're not likely to be interrupted, when you're feeling alert and there isn't anything pressing on the horizon, like a proposal due out the door by lunchtime. Sit down and ask yourself what you really would like to do, what different directions you'd like to take your business in, what would make you happy. Maybe look through the list of projects you completed last year and identify what you found interesting and what was less so. Perhaps that will steer you toward where you'd like to focus.

When you decide on something that you want to change, do differently, or embark on, you need a plan. How are you going to do it? When are you going to do it? What do you need to change to enable you to do it? I made a decision to cut my consulting efforts back to four days a week so I could sit down and write this book on Fridays. You gotta have a plan. Good luck!

What Is the Next Level?

The next level obviously means different things to different people. Generally it isn't something you should be too concerned with in your first few months of consulting. However, that isn't to say that you shouldn't be thinking about it. If the next level yields substantial benefits (if it doesn't, why would you bother with it?), it's something to aspire to. Just as there is no fixed definition of the next level, there is also no particular time when you should move to it.

When people talk about "the next level," they usually mean some sort of quantum jump or substantial change as opposed to general business growth. Some definitions of the next level are

- doubling your effective fee rate;
- creating another stream of income, perhaps by selling a product or information;
- opening an office in another country; or
- acquiring another business to double your business's size.

So what you regard as the next level for your business is very much a personal issue. However, you're in a consulting business for a number of reasons, so you should be continually exploring how you can improve your profit margin, make things easier for you, undertake more enjoyable work, and so on. So if you can work toward a quantum leap that helps you on your way, that's a very valuable thing to do.

A business coach once challenged me to find a way to charge out a junior consultant who worked for me at an effective rate of $1,000 an hour. I didn't succeed, but I did manage to get a rate of $700 an hour for her by selling work that she had done for one client to a number of clients with just a few minor changes.

The real challenge for me was finding a way to make that quantum leap. The key word is *leverage*. If you can find a way to leverage your time so that it works for you in multiples, you're well on the way to making that quantum leap. For example, if you charge people fifty dollars to listen to your webinar, you put in the same amount of effort whether ten people or a thousand people sign up.

One last point: There's no need to move to another level at all if you're happy where you are. I know lots of consultants who love doing what they do and are very satisfied with their current level of earnings. There's nothing wrong with that.

Vive la Différence!

Okay, you're setting up your own consulting company. Or you've already got it going, and the first projects are rolling in. Or maybe you're well established with a few years under your belt. Notice the common word in the previous sentences: *you.*

When we set up a business, be it consulting or any other, we have a number of ideas as to what we want. And, not surprisingly, these are usually drawn from our experience. Our experience derives from what we have seen, heard, been told, and learned at companies we've been exposed to. Consequently it's easy to end up with a clone of someone else's business (as described in chapter 2).

For example, if you're a naturally humorous, fun-loving person, that should show through in all aspects of your consulting business—from your website to the way you engage clients to how you treat staff or subcontractors. A very serious business approach that might pay dividends in another company would not be appropriate for you. And trying to copy the way other companies works would be compromising yourself in a way.

The point is that when you have your own business, it should be unique to you, a reflection of what you want, not a copy of what someone else wanted. And when you seek work out in the marketplace, you should be able to explain what's different about your company.

I explained unique selling points (USP) in chapter 6. A USP is certainly a market differentiator, but I mean something more fundamental here. You have the ability—the power, if you'd like—to fashion the business in a way that matches your ethos and reflects your character. This should run like a thread through everything you do in your business for as long as you continue to operate it.

For example, Peter is an excellent consultant who ran a profitable consulting business employing eight people. A year or so ago, he was looking for an exit strategy but felt that the "traditional route" of selling the business and riding off into the sunset wasn't something he would want to inflict on the boys and girls who worked for him.

"So don't do it," I advised him. "The business has always reflected your philosophy and ideals, so why should your exit strategy be any different?" In the end, he sold the business to a couple of his staff, probably for less than he could have been paid on the open market. However, he stayed true to his conscience and is happy as a result. The moral is, make it yours from start to finish.

CHAPTER 12

And Finally ...

Since you've made it this far, congratulations! I hear that statistically the average reader makes it to page eighteen in a book like this. (This says something about us, but I don't know quite what.) Anyway, thanks for your time, and I hope the journey has been worthwhile.

I plan to write a follow-up book that expands on the ideas in chapter 10, "Successful Strategies." I know there are a lot of small consulting companies struggling out there, and the book will be aimed at them. I intend to detail step-by-step processes for improving your sales success, increasing your fee rate, and generally turning your business around.

Finally, I would like to hear from you. The opinions and advice I've given in this book are all my own and are based on my experience. You may disagree or have other perspectives. Or you may just want to pass on an opinion or an experience, or provide some feedback. It's impossible to cover everything in a short book like this, and I would very much appreciate any comments you have. Please feel free to contact me at adrian@clearlead.ca or visit my website at www.adrianpartridge.com.

ABOUT THE AUTHOR

Adrian Partridge is the company president of ClearLead Consulting and has been consulting mostly on energy matters for many years. In that time, he covered almost everything from energy strategy for international industry to multifamily energy studies to municipality carbon footprints. He has completed carbon management and sustainability projects in eighteen countries around the globe and is one of the few people to have run energy-efficiency training courses in a Siberian brewery. He also has a strange tendency to struggle up the Grouse Grind (a seriously steep mountain trail near Vancouver, British Columbia) once a week.

He is married to Jennifer, has three sons, and lives in North Vancouver, British Columbia.

Printed in the United States
By Bookmasters